Audacious Acts of Successful Women

By Dawnna St Louis

To James, Brytt, Travian, Gloria and Sasha

52 Weeks of Audacity

52 Weeks of Audacity

ACKNOWLEDGEMENTS

Thank you:

To Sasha Rodriguez who is an E-Learning diva and supports my every move
(@ fusedlearning.com).

To Lois Creamer who helps speakers book more business and avoid costly errors
(@ BookMoreBusiness.com).

To Kimball Stadler who supports GURUS that want to have more exposure and spread their message while delivering a great amount of valuable information
(@ MountainTopUniversity.com).

To my hubby, my mommy, and my boys who said "Why not?".

To All the women and men (yes men) who shared story after story about the fantastic experiences, trials, and lessons of audacious women.

FROM THE AUTHOR

"Empower a woman; inspire a generation"
Dawnna St Louis

As the countdown begins to end one year and ring in another countless numbers of women make a multitude of resolutions; many of which surround being slimmer or looking younger or taking on the next big task. Many of these self-imposed promises are a throw-back from failed resolutions of years gone by.

So why do so many resolutions find their way into the stockpile of easily forgotten failures year after year? Simple, the New Year's resolution is not very resolute. We find ourselves repeating the failing pattern to make external changes because we have not yet made the internal changes necessary to make that happen.

The Audacious Acts of Successful Women is a way to provide you with the one tool that you need to fulfill your personal resolutions for a lifetime; YOU.

When you love the Diva in the mirror you will see less flaws in her and then you will take better care of her; when you have the nerve to stand up and speak out then you will have the courage to move forward; when you are ready to make a change then you will believe in yourself enough to follow your instincts and choose the best path.

The Audacious Acts are not something that you should consume in a day. This is a little weekly nudge outside of your comfort zone. If you struggle with a task then ask yourself why and when was the struggle the greatest. This is an area you may need to revisit. If you find a task easy, then support someone else that may need a little help.

Share the Audacious Acts of Successful Women with a friends, family, book club, or the AudaciousActs.com site for support and find yourself living a more bold, audacious and unapologetic life in a year.

Week 1: Stretch

Stretch

Although I had been speaking to business organizations for years, finding a place to practice and get real feedback was a struggle. The chick in the mirror could feedback that was a little too skewed towards perfection. I decided to join a local speakers association to solve my problem and give back. Upon membership acceptance, Angela volunteered to be my mentor so that I could get the most out of my membership.

About two months in Angela insisted that I compete in a humorous speaking competition. "With jokes like that Angela, you should enter," I chuckled, "I am a business speaker; I do PowerPoint with numbers, charts, and laser pointers. I don't do funny."

"The first contest is August," she said.

"I am not doing it," I replied.

"You will be fantastic. This is a teeny stretch for you," Angela continued as if I said nothing.

"You are like a cult member in desperate need of an intervention," I replied as she continued to ignore my rebuttals.

"Oh great! So you'll do it." Angela cheered.

Obviously she was hooked and desperately needed an intervention; and that would be the basis of my first funny speech. One day while practicing, I started to question myself, "What if I bomb? What if no one laughs? I would be failing in front of 500 people." I shook it off and thought "No one will die; no one will get hurt. What am I afraid of that I can't get over?" With my attitude in check I charged forward.

Not only did I win all five rounds of the competition, humor is a significant part of my career and is one of the reasons that I am consistently re-hired.

Imagine what would happen if I let the "What ifs" keep me from stretching just a little. What "what ifs" are slowing you down?

Take Action

Listen a little closer to your thoughts this week. Those same little "What If" gremlins in our head may initially start off as cute and sweet and cuddly as they make sure that we are prepared. But if you feed them after midnight and get water on them they turn into a real nightmare keeping us caged in and unable to stretch.

The next time that you are asked to stretch a little, go for it. Ask yourself "What is the worst that could happen?"

Enter a contest or competition, sing Karaoke, connect with someone on your bucket-list; but try something out of your comfort zone this week. Your goal is to stretch into the unknown.

Week In Review

My greatest challenge this week was:

_____

_____

_____

_____

My greatest success this week was:

_____

_____

_____

_____

I was most challenged when:

_____

_____

_____

_____

I am most proud of:

_____

_____

_____

_____

Week 2: The Middle

Get out of the Middle

Lisa had worked for the same company for 12 years when they laid her off. In fact, of the four of us Lisa was the only one that stayed. Gibby, Nina, and I had all taken classes to increase our knowledge, volunteered to gain experience; and moved up the ladder as quickly as we could before finding boredom and the lack of challenge as a regular part of our conversations. So one-by-one each of us left for better opportunities. In fact my next opportunity put me on path to be a C-Level executive.

Lisa, however, expected the company to pay for her classes; provide her with opportunities to use that knowledge; and then pay her for the privilege. She showed up on time; did her job; and stayed in the middle. The issue with the middle is that it gets crowded. Although Lisa did not do anything wrong at work; she neglected the most important stakeholder at the board meeting; Lisa.

Lisa forgot that is was her job; not her job's job, to make sure that she was educated, protected, and prepared for the future.

"My belief is that it is not the job of my employer to ensure that I am educated and ready for the future. That is my job.

Even if all I do is learn a new word, my goal is to be better every day and to learn and master something new every day.

It is one of the most effective ways that I have stayed light years ahead of the curve."

Dawnna

Take Action

Companies like steady. Steady people don't rock the boat and are like cogs in the wheel. They are reliable and do whatever it is that cogs do. The issue is that wheels change and cogs get smaller, cheaper, and more streamlined. Eventually cogs are no longer needed.

I am NOT telling you to leave your company or stop doing what you do. I am telling you to recognize that you have potential to grow or be so good at what you do that they can't live without you.

Consider how you can bring more value to the table:

- What topic will you master this year?

- What 4 major items will you learn?

    - Item 1 is for Q1, Item2 for Q2, etc.

- What is the most effective way for your to consume this new knowledge? (I listen to audio CDs while on planes and driving)

- What opportunities do you have to apply it? Hint: Volunteer.

- How can you apply this new knowledge and provide more value?

Week In Review

My greatest challenge this week was:

_____

_____

_____

_____

_____

My greatest success this week was:

_____

_____

_____

_____

_____

I was most challenged when:

_____

_____

_____

_____

_____

I am most proud of:

_____

_____

_____

_____

_____

Week 3: Don't Know

Don't Know

Remember when you were 16 and you knew *everything*! Although your favorite phrase was "I know"; your parents could have stricken those two words from your vocabulary forever. They knew that you did not know everything, even if you knew that you did.

As the saying goes, "The more we know, the more we know we don't know." As we age and recognize that we are actually clueless, we start searching for and consuming knowledge. This new version of us is quite different from the teenage version that had all of the answers.

Sometimes people don't actually grow out of the "I know" state. I found this out from my client Dave that *knows everything*. I find this is interesting because I am his presentation coach,

which means that he may not *know everything;* at least not about delivering a great speech.

Over the years that we have been together he has moved from severe stage fright to comfort on the platform. His content is amazing; however, when he tries to "wing it" he slips back into some pretty bad habits. For example, he turns into a human metronome and paces from stage left to stage right. One day I checked his shoes for notes because they were getting more eye-contact than his audience.

When I would bring up the issues he would say "I know"; but in fact he didn't know. He did not know how to see the correction, make the correction, and stick with the correction.

In fact, I would dare say that we have been working together longer than most, not because of my witty banter and great sense of humor, but because his "I know" blinders keep him from seeking out the information that he really needs to know.

Take Action

Of course you know what you know and may not know what you don't know. Interestingly enough you can't "un-know" what you do know.

Sometimes "knowing" causes us to miss out on valuable information. This usually happens during conversations. For example: We may start forming opinions before the other person is done speaking. We do this because "we know" what they are going to say next.

This week's exercise is a tough one. I honestly struggle with it regularly.

- Reduce the forming of opinions before a person is done speaking. Instead focus on the information and take mental notes.

- Take 3 full seconds after they have finished speaking before responding. When you start talking, first summarize what they have said using your mental notes from step 1.

- Remove the phrase "I know" from your vocabulary this week. When you feel the phrase falling from your lips say "Can I restate that to make sure that I understand?"

Week In Review

My greatest challenge this week was:

_____

_____

_____

_____

_____

My greatest success this week was:

_____

_____

_____

_____

I was most challenged when:

_____

_____

_____

_____

I am most proud of:

_____

_____

_____

_____

Week 4: SuperWoman

SuperWoman

The modern-day SuperWoman has a tendency to do it all. SuperWoman can bring home the bacon, fry it up in a pan, work all day, go to school at night, keep the house immaculate, and still look like a fantastic Diva. Meanwhile, she has not gone to the doctor, the gym, or just taken a mental health day for some "me time". SuperWoman sets the bar so high that SuperMan gets vertigo and a nosebleed. She is everyone's hero.

You can find SuperWoman putting in long hours, taking care of everything from the bills to the dinner to the yard work, and might periodically hear her complain about a lack of sleep or back pains; but don't count on it. She rarely asks for help and hasn't gone to the doctor for a check-up in years (although her family has).

On the outside, SuperWoman's cape is pristine and her hair is amazing (even in all that wind), but on the inside she needs some real care. The arch nemesis of SuperWoman is Reflecto. Reflecto looks exactly like SuperWoman and can only be seen in the mirror. Reflecto knows SuperWoman's weakness is the needs of everyone else.

Are you SuperWoman? Do you know one?

Take Action

It's time to put away the cape, take off the tights, and put *you* first. As a reformed SuperWoman your first job is to make sure that you are OK. Go to the doctor, the gym, or take some mental health time; but look out for you.

Next teach someone to take a task off your plate that takes up at least four hours per week. Other people can put dishes away; wash and put away laundry; do a report, etc. If you are worried that the whites will be pink, then have them wash darks. If you are worried that the dishes aren't stacked perfectly, then get over it. It's not that serious. Do you really want your biggest accomplishment to be "Dishwasher Stacker of the Year"? Give someone else the tools to do It better than you did and in their own style.

Finally; let go of perfection in place of profit. This doesn't mean that you should fall into slobbery; but perfection can waste time. I am sure there are misspellings in this book. It does not mean that my team didn't edit; however, it still went to print, you are still reading it, and I am still profitable.

Now it's your turn.

Week In Review

My greatest challenge this week was:

_____

_____

_____

_____

_____

My greatest success this week was:

_____

_____

_____

_____

_____

I was most challenged when:

_____

_____

_____

_____

_____

I am most proud of:

_____

_____

_____

_____

_____

Week 5:Manners

Manners

Gina D was struggling to move up the corporate ladder after 20 years of service the insurance firm. She was smart, dedicated, and loved her team; but time and again, Gina herself passed over for promotions by less qualified resources with less tenure.

During a 360 review, in which every resource that works with Gina has an opportunity to give confidential feedback, she was noted as competent but weak. Resources did not think Gina would stand up for them, while others said that she had no voice. Gina was in shock and decided to make a change.

During our initial conversation Gina started the conversation with, "Hi Dawnna. I am sorry for bothering you. My name is Gina and Lisa said that you could help me. I think I might need help because something is wrong with me ..."

Within the first three sentences of the conversation Gina had apologized, admitted that something was wrong with her, and said that she needed help. She apologized 18 times. Gina never gave herself a pat on the back or accepted a complement.

Gina needed to make but one apology; and that was to the woman in the mirror. She's probably the only person that truly deserves one. "Apologize for taking her strength and relegating her to the back of the line. Apologize for making her responsible for actions of others . Look her in the eyes and say, 'I'm sorry for saying sorry when I have nothing to be sorry for,'" I said, "And then forgive yourself."

Within three months Gina demanded another 360 review. She said "When I first started changing, people complained. They knew that I was no longer a push over and that I would press for the excellence that I deserved." Her 360 did a 180 and she is up for promotion.

Take Action

Overly apologetic people come off as weak, inadequate, and ineffectual. The words "I'm sorry" can shine a yellow-bellied spotlight on your persona and make others feel like they can take advantage of you. It's like greasing up the rungs of the corporate ladder before taking a step up in your stilettos. You are bound to take a painful fall.

For clarity: If you are responsible for causing hurt, then by all means, use good manners; otherwise let the phrase "I'm sorry" find silence before falling from your lips.

Before apologizing count to five and ask yourself these three questions:

- Am I responsible for causing hurt?
- Does this action deserve an apology?
- Am I sincerely sorry?

Get Help:
- Ask close friends to privately point out when you are overdoing it.

- Replace "I'm sorry" with another phrase such as "That's unfortunate".

Week In Review

My greatest challenge this week was:

_____

_____

_____

_____

My greatest success this week was:

_____

_____

_____

_____

I was most challenged when:

_____

_____

_____

_____

I am most proud of:

_____

_____

_____

_____

Week 6: Commit

Commit

Since the percentage of women-owned businesses that reach $1 million or more in annual revenue stands at just 1.8% of all private companies, compared with 6.3% for men owned firms**; it seems that showing up would be the first step towards success.

But statistics show that most women struggling with success also struggle with showing up on a consistent basis.

The ugly truth is that if you invite 20 women to an event; 10 will commit, 3 will show up & only 1 woman will be on time. Conversely, if you invite 20 men to an event; 15 will confirm, 12 will show up & only 2 will be more than 15 minutes late.**

The people that showed up early/on-time were more successful in business and tended to network with other successful business people for most of the event.

Since these birds of a feather flock together, it is time to get a new boa!

*We are talking about meetings external to a workplace or workplace where attendance is optional
*Babson College's Center for Women's Leadership

22

Take Action

Eager Commitments equals Over Commitments:

Do not instantly commit! Sometimes we are so eager to be people pleasers that we instantly say "YES!" Take the necessary time to check your calendar before making a decision. This should not take more than 30-60 minutes, unless you need to check with someone else. The moment that you make a decision let your hostess know. Don't wait until the deadline or day prior to the event. (That's just tacky!)

Get a friend: Networking buddies are the best way to ensure that you attend. Find someone that you can meet at the event. Determine ahead of time what to do if one of you is late. For example: I will go in after 15 minutes.

Set Up For Success: Add 3o minutes plus your tardy time to your event prep time. For example: If the event starts at 5pm and you usually start getting ready at 4pm but you are always 30 minutes late; then start getting ready at 3:00. Tip: Put 3:00 as the event start time in your calendar to reduce scheduling conflicts.

Week In Review

My greatest challenge this week was:

_____

_____

_____

_____

_____

My greatest success this week was:

_____

_____

_____

_____

I was most challenged when:

_____

_____

_____

_____

_____

I am most proud of:

_____

_____

_____

_____

Week 7: Value

Value

Jack is the owner of a well-known franchised networking group, He wanted to give Shelia the opportunity to create manuals about accounting practices for his paying members. He also wanted give her the chance to educate them about the giving how to manage their books themselves.

Jack said that he does not give many people the chance to have this kind of exposure to his market of 700 small business owners. To make sure that Shelia had a good crowd, he would only charge attendees $100 each and would only take 50% of the gross sales of Sheila's book.

"How generous!" said Barbara; one of the other high level volunteers in his organization as she began touting the wonders of this opportunity.

At just that moment Sheila started to wonder if the universe had flipped on its head. "This is a "For Profit" organization in the business of making money. In fact, Jack makes $74 million every year. Does he seriously think that I am going to work for free for a FOR PROFIT organization? That is the definition of 'hustling backwards'. Somewhere in someone's mind they think that I am going to pay them to work for them.   Are they crazy or did the 'I AM MORE STUPIDER TODAY' tattoo get stamped on my forehead?"

Before she knew it Sheila blurted out, "I don't work for free for 'For-Profit' organizations. Furthermore, time is finite and money is infinite. So you might have all the money in the world; but not all of the time. This means that my time is extremely valuable. Working for free to ensure that you have more money is not how I value my time and I am insulted that you would think otherwise."

Jack made Sheila a lucrative offer which included profit sharing after she delivered her Value Based Proposal. He recognized that her knowledge and expertise was very valuable.

Take Action

This week you will recognize your value and be prepared to expect and get what you are worth. This will take a few baby steps but they are definitely doable.

1. Determine your value. If you are struggling with this then consider your previous salary and add 100%. Now you have a range.
   Note: *If you are uncomfortable then ask yourself: "Why don't you deserve it."*

2. When someone asks you to do something for free say

"Time is Finite and Money is Infinite. What is your budget?"

3. You can do the work "Gratis" if:
   A: They will barter your value at double your rate: Marketing, Sales, other services, etc.
   B: They will introduce you to 5 future "paying" customers to whom they will regularly promote your services.

4. When you say your rate simply "say it" and then be quiet. Try to remove the "but I can discount" and "I am negotiable" after your rate.

5. Demand what you are worth.

Week In Review

My greatest challenge this week was:

_____

_____

_____

_____

_____

My greatest success this week was:

_____

_____

_____

_____

_____

I was most challenged when:

_____

_____

_____

_____

_____

_____

I am most proud of:

_____

_____

_____

_____

_____

_____

Week 8: Martyr or Hero

Martyr or Hero

Flight 429 ran into severe weather much to the discontent of every passenger, but none more so than Evelyn Green. She hated flying and constantly thought about the 5 minute Flight Safety seminar. For years she wondered "What would I do in that situation? I bet people would appreciate my efforts and consider me a hero!"

Well, that situation was here and Evelyn was ready to jump into action. The turbulence was so bad, that the air masks had fallen from their compartments and dangled in front of passenger's faces like the final lifeline on a treacherous journey. The flight attendant started to speak to the cabin of passengers; but Evelyn had already donned her hero's cape. "Pull the air mask down and tighten" she thought.

She noticed that several other passengers were unprotected by their masks. Although stricken with panic, desperately needing to sit down, and feeling as though she was losing oxygen Evelyn leaped from her seat and raced to help a child; then forced the mask on his mother; and continued her journey to save others although she was unprotected.

Just as she reached to help another passenger Evelyn felt a rush of electricity fill her body and then collapsed to the floor. During Evelyn's TV News Interview she said "I hope they appreciate all I have done and sacrificed for them. I put my life on the line to save others and I would do it again."

The news anchor followed with "Amazingly, this woman still has no idea that the masks fell accidentally and was asked to remain seated with her seatbelt fastened on several occasions before the Air Marshal found it necessary to Taser her. Many people are upset with her actions which forced an emergency landing. They wondered why she just did not take care of herself, follow Flight Safety instructions, and sit down."

Take Action

Some days, I will admit that wearing the SuperWoman outfit is pretty cool. The extra tight tights make my thighs look amazing and the cape keeps my ample butt from coming into view; but then Halloween is over and the costume goes back into the closet.

There is nothing wrong with helping others after you have helped yourself. You cannot give others strength or support if you have not ensured that you are strong.

It's time to take off the cape, climb down from the cross, and take action because you believe it is the right thing to do; not just because you expect others to notice.

◊ What three things can you do to do to put you first?

◊ Why are you doing those things? Is it for attention or for your well-being? Make sure that you are doing it for the right reason. Feed your ego while you take care of yourself.

◊ What do you expect the outcome to be?

Week In Review

My greatest challenge this week was:

_____

_____

_____

_____

I was most challenged when:

_____

_____

_____

_____

_____

My greatest success this week was:

_____

_____

_____

_____

I am most proud of:

_____

_____

_____

_____

_____

Week 9: Perspective

Perspective

At 19 years old I was living in my car on the border of North and South Carolina. I was searching for something more in life than heartbreak and loss; and driving from South Florida to somewhere else seemed like a great start.

With $50 in my pocket, I headed out on a fearless journey to somewhere else and although I was willing to go the distance my car was not. At the border of North Carolina it stopped working. Some part that was significantly more expensive than the remaining $20 in my pocket decided that it was no longer going to function.

Hours turned into days; days into weeks; and weeks into months. I was lucky enough to break down near a police station. The officers knew that I was living in my car and looked out for me. They let me wash their cars on pay day for extra cash. When I would win local talent contests for money, they would make sure that I got back to my car safely. On a rare occasion I would sleep in a hotel so I could enjoy a bathtub. But mainly I would brush up at a McDonalds and shower at a local YWCA.

I rarely tell this story and when I did my friend said, "I had no idea that you were homeless!"

With a furrowed brow I told her "I never said that I was homeless. I had a roof over my head; felt safe; and a place to sleep. I was protected by police officers 24x7 and came and went as I pleased. I wasn't homeless; I was free and grateful for everything I had!"

Sometimes life is a matter of perspective.

Take Action

I don't tell that story for people to feel sorry or impressed; in fact had it not been for my editor it would not make it in the book because to me it is a non-event. The story made it in the book to explain how critical perspective is to success and how focusing on what you have is critical to getting what you want.

Homeless or Free

I saw myself as having a roof over my head, a place to sleep a night and store my stuff (the trunk), and the safety of the local police. Besides allowing me to use their facilities, the local police also helped me get back to my car when contests would end late, they told others about me, and opened the door for opportunities.

I had the ultimate in freedom to come and go and live and grow my talent without worry or constraint. This positive perspective on the world has been one of my biggest keys towards success.

Take this week and take a closer look at your life. Instead of looking at what you don't have; everyday write a full page of gratitude for what you do have. Find the rose in the ashes.

Week In Review

My greatest challenge this week was:

_____

_____

_____

_____

My greatest success this week was:

_____

_____

_____

_____

I was most challenged when:

_____

_____

_____

_____

_____

I am most proud of:

_____

_____

_____

_____

_____

Week 10: Consume

Consume

and only one person would finish it. In fact our motivation to read a book after the purchase drops about 97%.

The number one way to increase knowledge and stay ahead of the competition is to read non-fiction books; while fiction books have been known to improve your imagination.

I was not an avid reader; however, I have always been a great consumer of information. I would listen to audio books, watch DVDs, browse the web, and would participate in anything that would increase my knowledge. Just a year ago I cracked open my college math book and started doing the problems when I got bored.

But consuming information is worthless if it is not put into action. If you know how to give CPR but then just stand on the sidelines when you could help, then what is the point? If you don't share your knowledge then why bother gathering it?

My saying is, "Empower a woman; motivate a generation." Let's start with your personal empowerment.

According to a study by MSNBC if you were in a room of 100 people attending a conference 20 of the people would buy a book at the conference, five would start to read it,

Take Action

This week is all about gathering information, taking action, and sharing.

Step 1: Select your method.

There are tons of ways to take in information; audiobooks, DVDs, books, internet; etc. If you are stuck on what to learn first, then learn about your strengths using StrengthsFinder 2.0 or read the Science of Getting Rich (its free) or check out YOLO (my other book).

Step 2: Use the information.

Take action on the information by determining how you can implement it. First do something different in the morning. You can consider how to use your strengths; visualize your future; or break the barriers in your mind.

Step 3: Share the what you've learned.

The best way to learn is to teach. Take a moment and share the information with someone else and help them become more powerful.

Week In Review

My greatest challenge this week was:

_____

_____

_____

_____

My greatest success this week was:

_____

_____

_____

_____

I was most challenged when:

_____

_____

_____

_____

_____

I am most proud of:

_____

_____

_____

_____

_____

Week 11 : Coat

Coat

It was my 25th birthday on June 25 and in six days, along with my husband and two sons, I would be moving into my first home. As we did our final walk- through, I started reflecting on my journey to this home from the Hyundai Excel that I lived in when I was 19. I felt like saying "Wow! You have come a long way baby!"

I did not get there alone; there were several people that helped me along the way including this one lady gave me her coat:

It was a perfectly good coat that she took right off her back so I would not be cold during the winter while I slept in my car. It wasn't trash; she was wearing it and would have worn it the next day! She wasn't rich or living on a trust fund; she was just a woman that had a coat.

When I made it back to my apartment, I knew it was time to pay it forward. I called everyone in my phone book until I found someone; anyone that I could help. My friend Lisa told me about Pamela G that had lived in a battered women's shelter and had just gotten the keys to her new apartment. She and her two sons were finally free of the abuse and were moving forward. I told Pamela that I would pay for a truck rental and she could have any and all of the furniture in the house; but she had to come over on June 30th to get it.

Pamela showed up with her two sons and several strapping men. She said, "When you say any and all; what do you mean? Are you crazy or rich?"

I told that I thought this was the least that I could do. After the men loaded up the truck, Pamela and her cohorts helped me clean the apartment until it was spotless. She then squeezed me in an embrace that almost broke my heart. Pamela was so grateful to have an apartment full of furniture; but she gave me the gift of being able to help someone.

Before she left she said, "You are not rich. You don't have new furniture coming so this is not trash, and I don't owe you anything. Why are you doing this?"

I said, "I didn't know it until now; but sometimes you have to give away a coat to appreciate being warm."

Take Action

It is really easy to give away something that you no longer use; from old shoes to old clothes; but when you have something that you are using right then, the difference is quite dramatic.

At that moment, you are not giving away trash; you are giving away treasure. Money is an easy way out; too easy. Lots of people swipe a credit card and give blindly to a charity; but their actions never touch their heart.

This week ask yourself how can you make a true change in someone's life. How can you give

something that is valuable to you and then not question how that item is used?

What do you have today that you take for granted but someone else would treasure?

NOTE: This is not trash! This is something that you might use on a regular basis?

Who can you give it to that could use it and would owe you nothing? Preferably someone that you won't see everyday.

The goal is to give freely without thought of how the item will be used.

Week In Review

My greatest challenge this week was:

_____

_____

_____

_____

_____

My greatest success this week was:

_____

_____

_____

_____

_____

I was most challenged when:

_____

_____

_____

_____

_____

_____

I am most proud of:

_____

_____

_____

_____

_____

_____

Week 12: Heart

Heart

You are competing against nine other people to sell Project Management Consulting services, and just like the nine other guys, you have a brochure filled with the results of your project management consulting work.

All this work does not mean that you will get hired. You need the other half of the equation. The funny thing about using the results of your work as a selling tool is that most people get stuck there. It might get you in the door; but it won't always close the deal.

If you plan to move up in your career, then you have to build a relationship that is based on being known, liked, and trusted. The good news is that it does not take a year for this to happen and you probably won't have to date for too long either.

If you pay close attention to your economic buyer and ask the right questions;

you could find yourself closing this deal, getting hired, or leveraging for more business faster than you thought.

The key is to find out what happens to the economic buyer on a personal level if you don't deliver. Most people say "But I will deliver." I am sure that you will. But the question is what happens to the buyer if you don't? You want to know what she has to lose on personal level. Ask smart questions such as:

- How will a successful project reflect on you? (Better reputation? More trust?)
- Who is depending on you and why?
- Tell me about a similar project to this one and the outcomes for the stakeholders. How are they viewed in the organization?
- What would have happened if they failed/ succeeded? Is that a concern on this project?

The answers to these questions allow you to position yourself as a partner that really cares about the delivering the results as well as ensuring the economic buyer succeeds.

Take Action

This week is about stepping in to the shoes of your economic buyer. Regardless of whether you own your own business or not; there is someone that has something to lose (other than money or a job) if you fail. That is your economic buyer.

Step 1: Define who the economic buyer is in your situation. This is the person that is relying on your amazing results. They trust you. It could be the person hiring you or counting on you.

Step 2: Find out the personal negative and positive results associated your delivery. Will their reputation be tarnished if you fail; Will they be a superstar if you succeed; Will they lose respect; Will they gain a promotion; Will they no longer be trusted; Will they garner the respect of their peers?

Step 3: Create a message that addresses not only the results of your work; but also her personal concerns. When communicating make sure that you address both results and concerns. This will move you much higher than your competition and make you a trusted resource for future solutions.

Week In Review

My greatest challenge this week was:

_____

_____

_____

_____

_____

My greatest success this week was:

_____

_____

_____

_____

_____

I was most challenged when:

_____

_____

_____

_____

_____

_____

I am most proud of:

_____

_____

_____

_____

_____

_____

Week of
Reflection

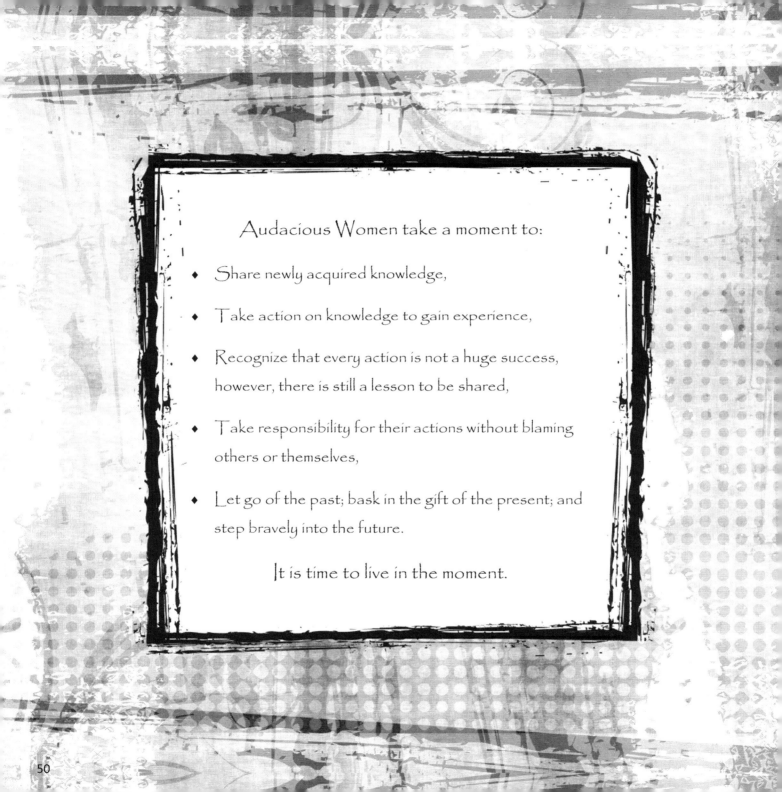

Audacious Women take a moment to:

♦ Share newly acquired knowledge,

♦ Take action on knowledge to gain experience,

♦ Recognize that every action is not a huge success, however, there is still a lesson to be shared,

♦ Take responsibility for their actions without blaming others or themselves,

♦ Let go of the past; bask in the gift of the present; and step bravely into the future.

It is time to live in the moment.

Reflection

My biggest accomplishment was:

_____

_____

_____

_____

_____

What surprised me about myself was:

_____

_____

_____

_____

_____

I am the proudest of myself because:

_____

_____

_____

_____

_____

What I plan to do differently is:

_____

_____

_____

_____

_____

Reflection

What have you learned about yourself?

_____

_____

_____

_____

_____

The toughest action was:

_____

_____

_____

_____

_____

I have shared my new knowledge with:

_____

_____

_____

_____

_____

The week that I will retry is:

_____

_____

_____

_____

_____

Week 14: PRS

Procrastination Reduction System
Or Personal Reliability System (PRS)

You have been waiting all week for Sandra to get back to you like she said she would. It's been 4 days and you just can't stand it anymore. You finally call her to get the status, only to hear the words "Oh! I forgot" or "My bad. Something came up."

My favorite part is when they start telling you about the other things that came up that were way more important than you. The whole time you're thinking, "Great! Not only do <u>you</u> think I'm not important; now you want convince <u>me</u> that I'm not important too."

Follow up is critical to success and forgetting that you promised to follow up is an insult.* We all have good intentions; but the impact of not getting back to someone as promised could be detrimental to a great business or personal relationship.

You have just stacked yourself in the pile of unreliable people that never do what they say they were going to do, regardless of how innocent the oversight. No one is perfect but this is one area where we want to strive for it.

The sad thing is that most of us have a Procrastination Reduction System or Personal Reliability System (PRS) that we only use as a cell phone or to take pictures of that weird guy doing that weird thing in his car.

With the advent of the smart phone we can update our calendars, set reminders, connect people, and do so much more than just store funky pictures and call our friends to tell them about it.

*Sometimes emails get lost in your junk folder or never find their way to our email at all. In that case a person can call and confirm and not assume that you are a loser, unless you have a history.

Take Action

The goal is to be at peace with your actions and promises. There is nothing worse than remembering that you forgot to do something for someone when they are standing in front of you. Instead of scrambling for excuses be prepared to accolades.

Making Connection: When you agree to connect two people, do it instantly. Take a moment to send a text/email to both.

Coffee/Call: The next big dropped ball is a call or coffee appointment that you promise to do "next week" but never actually get around to. To overcome this hurdle schedule the time on your calendar using your smart phone immediately.

Information: Finally, there is the delivery of information. The first rule is to never agree to deliver something that you have not already developed. If you have developed it, leverage a service like DropBox and send it instantly from your smart phone; otherwise, shift responsibility back to the requestor. Simply ask the person to send you an email or calendar invite requesting the data they want and when they want it.

Week In Review

My greatest challenge this week was:

_____

_____

_____

_____

_____

My greatest success this week was:

_____

_____

_____

_____

_____

I was most challenged when:

_____

_____

_____

_____

_____

I am most proud of:

_____

_____

_____

_____

_____

Week 15: LOL

LOL

"When I was working as a techy there was a manager that had the best laugh. She would toss her head back and open her mouth as if she were letting the heavens in on the joke. Her full bodied laugh was contagious and existed without inhibitions or concerns of consequence. She seemed to smile all the time; I wondered if it was because of her laugh.

I see some women that cover their mouths and chuckle as if perfectly trained Geishas; and other women use alcohol as an excuse to laugh out loud then claim amnesia to their reckless abandon. Who needs an excuse for a great laugh?"

Dawnna

In the movie "The Color Purple" Whoopi Goldberg's character, Celie, gets a laugh out loud lesson. Celie places her hands to her mouth and clinches her lips when she smiles or laughs to hide her smile and muffle the sound.

During this laugh lesson, her friend makes a joke, flips Celie around to the mirror and presses her hands by her side forcing Celie to see the reflection of the smiling woman in the mirror. Eventually Celie gives up and laughs without apprehension. The shackles on her smile and laugh were finally released. Celie could do something never before attempted; she could laugh out loud and be proud of it.

What freedom she must have felt for the first time in her life.

This week we will remove the shackles from your laugh and your smile. This week you will find your own inner beauty in your smile, your voice, and your laughter.

Take Action

We all know that laughter is the best medicine; but how many times do we really just LAUGH?

Step One: Laugh Alone: Watch a movie that really tickles your funny bone. When something funny happens laugh... OUT LOUD! When people are alone they tend to think something is funny, but they don't laugh. This week laugh for you.

Next: Laugh with Friends: Go out with some fun friends and without a drop of alcohol in your system laugh as hard as you can; as loud as you can. Take note that people will start laughing with you. Laughing brings up the endorphins and all the stories will get funnier and funnier.

Final Challenge: Laugh for no reason at all: This is the most fun. When you are with someone, start laughing out loud for no reason at all or at something inconsequential. Then laugh at the fact that they are laughing and have no idea why. When asked why you were laughing simply say "I have no idea." You will be surprised that you will start laughing again.

Week In Review

My greatest challenge this week was:

_____

_____

_____

_____

_____

My greatest success this week was:

_____

_____

_____

_____

I was most challenged when:

_____

_____

_____

_____

_____

I am most proud of:

_____

_____

_____

_____

_____

Week 16: AA

Accuracy and Availability

Joshua needed to turn in the month end numbers like he was supposed to at the end of every month. Tara, his manager, spent a significant amount of time training him and ensuring that he was clear on what needed to be done, that he had the tools to do the work, and understood the value of his work.

As Tara started checking her list; She already knew that on Monday morning Joshua would not have those numbers and if he did, they would be inaccurate. Tara was one to educate, delegate and release; but babysitting was not on her task list.

After Joshua turned in inaccurate numbers for a third month in a row, Tara retrained Joshua along with the new intern Margie. When Tara would ask for the first draft of the numbers Margie would respond within 5 minutes while Joshua would never respond or have an excuse for the numbers not being available.

When the duo turned in their individual reports, initially Tara would recheck Margie's numbers against Joshua's for accuracy. She recalled sitting for several hours trying to figure out what was wrong with Margie's numbers only to realize that it was Joshua's work that was simply incorrect.

After a while, Tara used Margie's report. She knew that she could trust the data and it would be turned in on time. Soon she promoted Margie; and although Margie had only been employed for less than a year Tara really liked and trusted her.

She did not feel the same way about Joshua .

Based on the story do you like Joshua more than Margie? Probably not. Accuracy increases trust while availability increases likeability. For anyone to get in your corner and support you, they must know, like and trust you. Accuracy and availability are the fastest ways to turn a customer into a fan.

Take Action

If your bank balance was a range instead of an accurate amount down to the penny, would you still trust your banker with your money? If your funds were not available for use, would you like your bank? Probably not.

For your customers to like and trust you, you must be as accurate and available as you expect your bank to be with your money.

Your network must know, like and trust you in order to

become fans. This week concentrate on being accurate and available. Consistently serving your customers this double dose of service will ensure that they like and trust your more.

- When does your network need your information or attention the most?

- How can you make the most often requested information readily available?

- How can you work towards being more accurate on a more consistent basis?

- What areas need more attention?

Week In Review

My greatest challenge this week was:

_____

_____

_____

_____

_____

I was most challenged when:

_____

_____

_____

_____

_____

My greatest success this week was:

_____

_____

_____

_____

_____

I am most proud of:

_____

_____

_____

_____

_____

Week 17: Tools

Tools

My goal was to create great videos with great content for my audience in the most economical; but most professional fashion possible. I converted a room into a studio; leveraged my iPhone 4s as a video camera; rigged a tripod for it to sit on; and purchased a Senheisser professional microphone. I estimated that this project would only take a couple of hours.

After five hours of recording I learned that if you use the front facing camera on the iPhone 4s it records in standard definition and I wanted high definition and the audio didn't work that well. "Damn!," I thought, "back to the drawing board."

It was a week later and I was still recording for various reasons. First, there is a hum in the audio because of the amplified power to the microphone, then there were lighting issues, and then my hair looked funky. Because I possess bullheaded determination, I would not give up; but neither would this cycle of errors. My "quick" five hour recording project turned into five weeks.

One afternoon my husband, James, hands me two gift wrapped boxes that read "For James". I said, "Why are you giving these to me; they are obviously you." "Yep; just open them," he replied.

In one box was an HD Camera that allows for an external microphone attachment; and a lighting kit and backdrop in the other box. "Wow! Honey thanks," I said as I gave him the requisite kiss and raced off like a kid with a new toy. After 5 hours of recording and editing I had 10 perfect videos. Then it occurred to me; the box read "For James".

I said, "Honey, how is this for you?"

He replied, "If you are using the right tools to do the job then you can finish your work in five hours and I get to spend time with my 'happy' wife; which is way better than spending time with the non-productive, frustrated, bitchy one that I have had for the past five weeks. You're Welcome."

Point taken.

Take Action

It is time to get beyond getting by.

It is OK to use a butter knife to take out a quick screw, but not to put together a wall unit or rebuild an engine.

This week take a moment to look at what you are you doing to get by and how that is affecting your end result.

Are you spending more time than necessary?

Are you wasting money?

Are you doing extra work?

Look at how you can stop getting by and start getting done.

This does not mean that you have to spend lots of money. I could have easily rented the equipment or borrowed/bartered it.

It is time to get beyond your current status ,enjoy better results and more of your valuable time.

Week In Review

My greatest challenge this week was:

_____

_____

_____

_____

_____

My greatest success this week was:

_____

_____

_____

_____

_____

I was most challenged when:

_____

_____

_____

_____

_____

_____

I am most proud of:

_____

_____

_____

_____

_____

_____

Week 18: Socks

Socks

Brian owns a Social Media Company and wanted me to meet John Novac; a high-powered commercial real estate broker. John is a taller slimmer version of Alec Baldwin with a cheeky sense of humor. At the meeting, he was dressed in a Black Zegna suit, no tie, and red argyle socks with blue squares and black accents; which perfectly matched his blue faced watch with a black leather band and red stripes.

Brian hoped that I could say enough wonderful things about his business that John would finally sign on the dotted line. After talking with John for a few minutes; I learned that he brokered most of the deals that changed the Miami skyline, as well as, the community where my home sits. The conversation was like taking a tour down memory lane.

After talking and laughing for about an hour John ended the conversation with a complaint, *"People just don't write a letter or send a note; it's all electronic. I miss good conversations; thank you for this one."*

As we walked out to our respective cars those red argyle socks made their debut. I said, "John, I am digging the socks! I really like the way that they match your watch!"

"YEAH BABY! I'm bringing argyle back!" he waived his watch hand and let out hearty laugh before driving off.

After the meeting, I realized why Brian could not close the deal. Ten minutes into the conversation he took a phone call and never returned. He did not know John and did not give John and chance to know him. Brian just wanted John to sign on the dotted line.

About a week later during a shopping trip, I noticed a set of brightly colored argyle socks; one salmon; one green; and the other blue. I sent them to John in a box with red argyle gift wrap and a note that read, "For when you are feeling daring; For that big money deal; and For those rare conservative days. I hope that you have a watch to match them all. "

Four days later, John introduced me and the owner of a high powered C-Level development organization. Just so happens that they need someone like me to help leaders discover how to balance innovation with fiscal responsibility and time to market.

While the deal is worth a lot, those socks were priceless.

Take Action

Some people are detailed oriented while others are not. But the story is not about the details, as much as it is about people.

People work with people that they know, like, and trust. Not only was Brian not getting know John, he never gave John a chance to know him either.

This week is about getting to know your network outside of a business deal.

How well do you know someone? Here are questions to get you started.

How did you get started in your current business? What was your path?

What is your motivation? Why did you choose this business?

What do you value most in relationships?

If you could do anything outside of work, what would it be?

What did you want to be when you were little? Did you achieve that? Why or why not?

Week In Review

My greatest challenge this week was:

_____

_____

_____

_____

My greatest success this week was:

_____

_____

_____

_____

I was most challenged when:

_____

_____

_____

_____

_____

I am most proud of:

_____

_____

_____

_____

_____

Week 19: Excuses

Excuses

After talking to several successful women that dared to succeed beyond what was thought possible, they would always say, (usually with a big bellied laugh) "Maybe I was just too stupid to know better." Another said, "Or maybe I was just too smart to think that I could get away with accomplishing less." In the lives of Audacious Women excuses need not apply.

Degrees, certifications, and higher levels of education are irrelevant* to finding their passion and surpassing the bar.

The number one thing I heard from successful women was that there was never an excuse to produce less than something amazing; and there was always a reason to produce something that provided significant value.

They also had "BS excuse radar" that can be heard from miles away.

They sound like this:

- I'm too fat, skinny, short, sexy, ugly, <fill in your word here>
- I don't know . . .;
- What will people think;
- I did not go to school for that;
- I have no experience;
- I don't have enough money, time, resources, education, experience, etc.; T
- They will never pick or hire me; I'm afraid; scared; tired; alone; etc.

Audaciously Successful Women rarely, if ever, use these statements. If they do, it is a fleeting moment that turns into fuel for forward movement.

Remember: *You can be PERFECT or PROFITABLE. Don't let your reach for perfection cause you to miss out on prosperity.*

*Unless of course you will be performing surgery or some other type of practice requiring such education

Take Action

This week you will take a chance that you have not taken before. Work on being brave not perfect; just take a chance without excuses for failure.

If you hate to have pictures taken of you; then act like a supermodel and get in front of the camera. If you think that something is over your head; then get a book; learn about it; and speak like an expert on the subject. If you are afraid of the dark then stand in front of the abyss and yell back at the darkness.

This is a time to recognize that you can do anything that you set your mind to. The goal is to bite off a little more than you can chew but not enough to get choked.

Whatever the excuse this week, eradicate it and move forward.

If you are still nervous about taking a chance then ask yourself what is the worst that could happen. Come to terms with it and do it anyway.

Take note of the outcome: You are stronger and you did not die. Now, do it again tomorrow.

Week In Review

My greatest challenge this week was:

_____

_____

_____

_____

_____

My greatest success this week was:

_____

_____

_____

_____

_____

I was most challenged when:

_____

_____

_____

_____

_____

I am most proud of:

_____

_____

_____

_____

_____

Week 20: Chameleon

Chameleon

Who is your target market? If you had to determine one person that you were working towards having as a customer or stakeholder, who would that be? What does your perfect customer look like? Is it Oprah, Donald Trump, Bill Gates, etc.

These questions and many others are the bane of speakers, entrepreneurs, and people just looking for a job. New speakers tend to say, "I speak to everyone about everything," while entrepreneurs answer with, "This product is for everyone." Even people looking for a new opportunity will say "Anyone that will pay me a salary."

During a recent workshop the moderator responded by saying "Great! Get a phone book, start calling everyone and delivering solutions and services about everything."

Even when you look at super companies from Apple to McDonalds they also have a target market. McDonalds is not targeting vegans; and their initial target market has expanded over many years.

During its inception Facebook was only targeting college students attending a particular school; now they have hundreds of millions of users. Why does this question cause issue?

Because we don't want to cut ourselves out of a potential opportunity; we want to be available for everyone and leverage all of our skills. We want to be the like Chameleon and adapt our colors to the current environment or prospect. We want to be every solution to everyone.

The problem with being the Chameleon is that they adjust their colors for camouflage. Their goal is to hide from sight. Is that what you want to do with your business? Hide it from sight?

If you really want to reach your target market, then shed your Chameleon skin and be the right solution for your target market while remaining true to yourself.

Take Action

Consider what you do really well. *For example: I know how to move women into action.*

- If you are confused and unsure then check out StrengthFinders 2.0. Take the test to get your top 5 strengths. GREAT! Now you have a starting point.

Who would pay you to share this talent? *For*

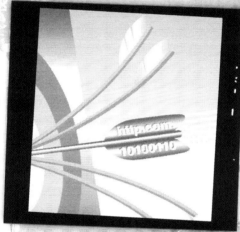

Example: Organizations like Clairol, MaryKay, Women's Associations would pay me to get women to take action. I could work with diversity teams in large corporations.

- How will you reach your target market? *For example: I can write a blog or book, tweet, send letters, become an expert, etc.*

- Who can you help and leverage to meet your goals? *For example: I can talk to some Not For Profits organizations and leverage their PR resources.*

Week In Review

My greatest challenge this week was:

_____

_____

_____

_____

_____

My greatest success this week was:

_____

_____

_____

_____

_____

I was most challenged when:

_____

_____

_____

_____

_____

_____

I am most proud of:

_____

_____

_____

_____

_____

_____

Week 21: Up

Up

The speaker at the front of a large and filled room asks for volunteers to sit in the hot seat. As a result the volunteer will likely get amazing value for publicly going under the microscope for a few moments.

Do you raise your hand, speak up, stand up, move up to the front, or just sit back hoping that you can blend in with the seat so that you are not seen? Do you have regret after watching what the person on the hot seat had the privilege of experiencing?

I attend 10 seminars per year at the Florida Speakers Association's monthly meetings with experts like Pegine Echevarria, Ford Saeks, Randy Gage, Joaquin DePosada, Lois Creamer, and many more.

These people are amazing experts, consultants, and coaches are at the top of their profession. Although the event is usually only about $50, I get way more than $50 worth of value. Not just because of their actions; but because of mine.

There are lots people that sit back, hope, and then regret. If you take a look at the bold women in the audience they usually find themselves fully engaged on stage, showered with benefits bestowed on them by experts, and took actions that would continue to propel them forward.

Those women take complete advantage of the opportunity. If you check their mindset at the door you will notice a few things about them:

- They sit up front
- They step to volunteer
- They speak up to answer questions (usually the speaker has to say "Let's give someone else a chance")
- They stand up to speak
- They walk up to the front when volunteers are requested (and usually before they are asked).

These women let nothing stop them from being *up* for the next opportunity.

Take Action

Step 1: Know "what" the expert will talk about and be prepared to ask them HOW to implement that expertise in your business. For example: Lois Creamer of Book More Business might tell you to create a positioning statement. Be prepared to ask her how.

Step 2: Get over "looking stupid" in front of an others. If that doesn't work then think "I will look a little stupid today to make a million tomorrow." Now stupid doesn't really seem that bad.

Step 3: Experts appreciate good participation. Get on the hot seat and get more value. Note: Don't try to outsmart the speaker and don't try to be the comedian; instead actively participate.

Step 4: Ask the expert for other free actionable information that will tell you HOW to proceed. Most will have free content on their website, webinars, videos, etc.

Step 5: Implement what you have learned and then give the expert credit for your newly found knowledge. They will appreciate it and will start to see you as an ally.

Week In Review

My greatest challenge this week was:

_____

_____

_____

_____

_____

My greatest success this week was:

_____

_____

_____

_____

_____

I was most challenged when:

_____

_____

_____

_____

_____

_____

I am most proud of:

_____

_____

_____

_____

_____

_____

Week 22: Who?

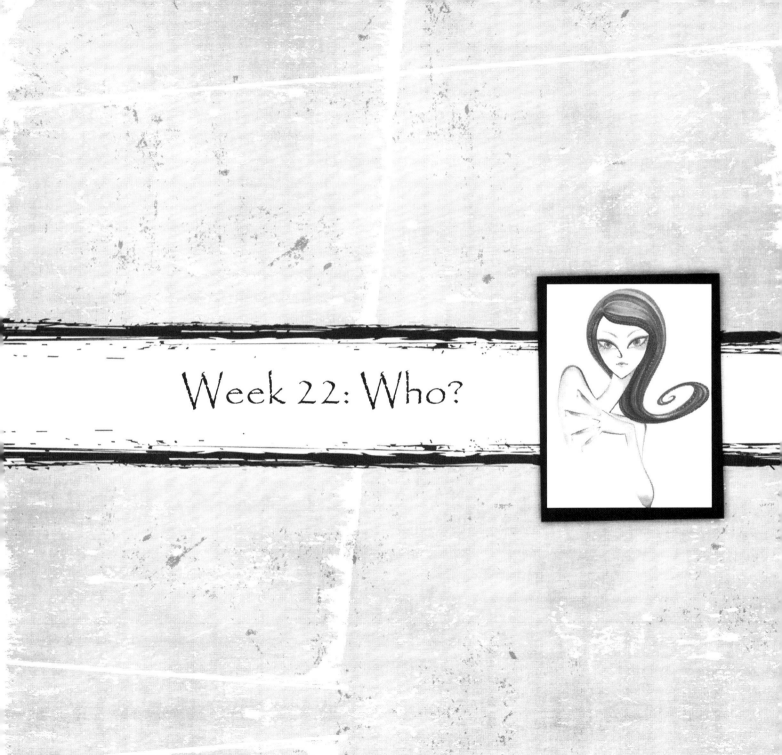

Who?

Melissa is a confident woman that is full of life. She is the type of person that speaks her mind, confronts issues immediately, and laughs through her day. Regardless of how great or bad things are, Melissa just handles them effortlessly. Her twenty years of technology experience combined with her ability to communicate at all levels propelled her up the corporate ladder. Melissa is a confident, beautiful, and brilliant force of nature.

Melissa and Nick were meeting for the first time. As Melissa exited her vehicle in front of the local Starbucks, Nick's facial expression transformed from happiness to sheepishness; and almost fear. "You must be Nick" Melissa exclaimed as she extended a firm handshake. Nick was sweating at this point and fearful of shaking Melissa's hand with his damp hand.

As the conversation continued and Nick got more comfortable, Nick admitted that he thought Melissa was very intimidating. "Really? What did I do?" she replied. "I think it was the way you came at me; the way you exited the car. You should have smiled more when you got out of your car"

Nick said.

Melissa started considering how she looked exiting her car. "Did he expect me to start grinning like a school girl from the moment I opened the door. Was I supposed to skip into the Starbucks?" she thought.

After considering the statement for a moment she told Nick "If I were a man would you have been intimidated?" He laughed and said "Of course not." Melissa replied " I don't think that I intimidated you, as much as you were intimidated by me. Why do you think you felt intimidated?"

Nick said "Because you look smart; you are beautiful; and I knew that I would have to bring my 'A-Game'."

"As compared to what? Your B, C or D game? Don't you always bring your A game?" asked Melissa.

Nick said, "When I am doing business with a man I do."

Take Action

	ME	
	OK	Not OK
THEM OK	We are good	It's my issue
Not OK	It's their issue	It's our issue

How many times have you been asked to be a little less or a little different for someone else to be comfortable?

Melissa did something amazing, she did not take responsibility for how someone else felt. She knew that she was OK; but Nick had issues to work on.

Take a look at the quadrant. When an issue comes up determine where the issue lies. In Melissa's situation, Nick tried to make intimidation Melissa's issue, when in actuality it was his problem.

Melissa did not need to change.

Week In Review

My greatest challenge this week was:

_____

_____

_____

_____

_____

My greatest success this week was:

_____

_____

_____

_____

_____

I was most challenged when:

_____

_____

_____

_____

_____

_____

I am most proud of:

_____

_____

_____

_____

_____

_____

Week 23: Impact

Impact

Brie sent an email to her top client, Dana Brek; an executive of the largest Marketing Management Company in the country. Brie's e-mail read:

Dana:

You sent me an e-mail on Thursday, March 5 requesting that I give you a date for deliverables. You also wanted additional services. When I spoke to you last I thought it was clear that we were not going to move forward until we could sort out the scope of work on your project. Your need to let me know when your calendar is open so that you can finally understand this.

Thanks!

The next day Dana canceled the contract and refuse further contact with Brie. Her note read:

Since I am having issues with clarity, I will move forward with someone that can communicate in a manner which is suitable for ME. You no longer have to worry about that. YOU need to understand that "Me, You and I" have no place in email correspondence.

Why was Dana done? Although Brie's intent was to explain that that the project could move forward once the scope of work was complete, the impact of her message was quite different. Read the email that Brie sent using the tone of a 6 year old girl. Sounds pretty innocent; right?

Now read the email putting significant emphasis on the words You, Me, and I. In fact, read it with an attitude (as if someone just stomped on your new Coach sandals).

See the difference?

The impact and the intent are quite different; however, you are judged on your impact not your intent.

Take Action

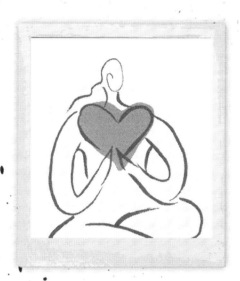

This recently happened to me. Jo wanted to meet Mary. To introduce Jo to Mary, I sent a simple text message. Mary responded to both Jo and I confirming the message. Jo later said "*You* never did what *you* said *you* were going to do. *You* did not send a text message." Taken aback by her tone and statements I said "You are right. Don't worry about it," then I told Mary ignore the text. Tone can break up marriages, so be careful with sarcasm, joke, and innuendo in an email.

Take a moment before sending any emails this week.

The first rule of being audacious is to have a positive impact. Make sure the impact of your message matches your intent. If you are angry, feel free to write the angry email as intended. BUT WAIT! Don't press send.

Now, take a moment to edit the email by removing the words "YOU", "ME", and "I". By the time you are finished your temper should have subsided and you will have an email that won't cause embarrassment later.

Week In Review

My greatest challenge this week was:

_____

_____

_____

_____

_____

My greatest success this week was:

_____

_____

_____

_____

I was most challenged when:

_____

_____

_____

_____

_____

_____

I am most proud of:

_____

_____

_____

_____

_____

_____

Week 24: Cash Cow

Cash Cow

When I was a little girl, my grandmother and I would walk to the corner grocery store to purchase the week's food supply for the family.

We lived well below middle class so counting coins was critical. Although I was only eight, I recognized my grandmother's grocery ritual and followed her through every step like a lost little puppy after a treat.

She kept a list on the refrigerator of items that were consumed during the week. This was her starting point, "Michael likes Fruity O's so we'll stay with those; but none of the kids liked pears so we will get less of those; but these little monkey's love bananas so we will get more of those." After creating a list that was checked and balanced, she put the approximate dollar amount of each item and added $5 to the list total. My job was to find the coupons that matched the items she planned to purchase.

In all those years my grandmother never wrote a check, she never went over (in fact she was usually within $1 of the final amount), and she never took more than $5 extra in the envelope with the grocery money. There was no ATM terminal just in case she was off by $10. The money that she did not spend went into her savings.

When my husband and I wanted to buy a house, I started thinking about my grandmother and the simplicity of it all. She never lived beyond her means and had a savings of $5-$10 per week that she had put away for years. My husband and I made significantly more money and fed significantly fewer people, but our savings account had $1 in it.

If we were going to get a house, we had to change. So I followed my grandmother's envelope system; "If we ain't got it in cash, we ain't spending it," I announced in the best southern voice I could muster. After getting over the initial plastic card withdrawal, we were really able to do this. We planned lunches, groceries, and dinners which trumped winging it and eating out all of the time. Within 30 days we both lost 5 pounds and gained $600 in our savings; something previously thought impossible.

Take Action

This one might take a little longer to really get a hold of than some of the other acts. But the payoff is amazing.

1. Put the ATM Card, Credit Card, and any other payment method other than cash away; far away.

2. Replace credit card purchases with cash purchases: Gas, Lunch, Coffee, Dinner, Meeting Fees, Groceries, etc. Create a budget and withdraw cash (yes the green stuff) from your account that equals the amount of normal weekly purchases.

3. On separate envelopes write

the amount of each item. For example: Lunch @ $10/day for 5 days. Envelope Total = $50.

4. Only spend the amount in the envelopes. Be careful swapping cash from one envelope to another. Gas money spent on a great lunch could get you stranded on the side of the road.

5. After 2 weeks consider where else you can save: I.e. Purchase lunch 3x per week and brown bag lunch 2x per week. $20 per week savings or $80 in your account.

Check your account at the end of the month.

Week In Review

My greatest challenge this week was:

_____

_____

_____

_____

_____

My greatest success this week was:

_____

_____

_____

_____

I was most challenged when:

_____

_____

_____

_____

_____

I am most proud of:

_____

_____

_____

_____

_____

Week 25: Marshmallows

Marshmallows

You are in row five; seat twelve stuffed right in between the lady with the giant purse and the guy that keeps hogging the armrest. You don't mind; after all you paid $995 for some great information that will transform your business.

The moderator makes her way to center stage and begins with a 20 minute dissertation of inconsequential conference history. Finally the speaker that you traveled half-way across the country to see is introduced.

His genius in the marketing and consulting field has been noted as the "Corporate Game Changer" and all of his books are on your book shelf. Those books described "THE WHAT"; what you should do like "Get more Facebook followers; create a compelling campaign; engage your audience". Today you are here to learn "THE HOW"; how to "get those Facebook followers; create a compelling campaign; and engage your audience".

As you ready your notepad and pen for golden nuggets that will drop from his lips and into your bank account, you focus intently. For 45 minutes you listen to every syllable; laugh at every joke; and never move your pen from that paper. After 46 minutes; you realize that you have written down nothing.

You fell into a strategically placed trap. The corporate game changer fed you marshmallows and for 45 minutes you ate them. Marshmallows taste good as you eat them; they may even give you a little endorphin rush; but after about 45 minutes you don't feel so good about consuming the whole bag. It was just FLUFF and FILLER; no real nutritional value; in fact right now you might feel a little sick.

This is becoming the BANE of the speaking and seminar world. "THE WHAT" is nothing more than a regurgitation of what is currently on the pages of the speaker's book along with their latest product and upcoming seminar; all that are available for purchase at the back of the room for another $995; Major Credit Cards are accepted.

You deserve and need "THE HOW". It's time to get it.

Take Action

If you really want to know HOW to do something you can go to the experts at a seminar trying to sell you a little more or you can take other actions:

Step 1: Create a mastermind group with people that will be willing to share info and support each other.

Step 2: Send letters asking your questions to several experts. Someone will answer.

Step 3: Interview an expert and then write an article about them. They LOVE this and you get your questions answered.

Week In Review

My greatest challenge this week was:

_____

_____

_____

_____

_____

My greatest success this week was:

_____

_____

_____

_____

_____

I was most challenged when:

_____

_____

_____

_____

_____

_____

I am most proud of:

_____

_____

_____

_____

_____

_____

Week of

Reflection

The Audacity to be Proudly Imperfect

Audacious women take action and strive for better without pausing for perfection.

Audacious women know that we can be perfect or profitable; but no one can be both.

Audacious women will strive for perfection and use profitability to consistently improve.

Audacious women know that profitability is more than just money. Profitability is beauty, time, outcomes, health, and the results of our hard work.

Reflection

What have you learned about yourself?

_____

_____

_____

_____

The toughest action was:

_____

_____

_____

_____

I have shared my new knowledge with:

_____

_____

_____

_____

The week that I will retry is:

_____

_____

_____

_____

Reflection

My biggest accomplishment was:

_____

_____

_____

_____

_____

What surprised me about myself was:

_____

_____

_____

_____

_____

I am the proudest of myself because:

_____

_____

_____

_____

_____

_____

What I plan to do differently is:

_____

_____

_____

_____

_____

_____

Week 27: Silence

Silence

Have you ever noticed that silence during a conversation, meeting, or any type of ongoing interaction can be uncomfortable for some. That need to fill in the void with anything other than more silence can be overwhelming.

There is power in that void of sound. Silence is one of the most powerful tools that we can use in communications; however, we don't leverage it often enough. The number one technique is to closing a deal is to, well, shut up.

I learned over the years that most sales people talk themselves out of a sale when they should be listening themselves into a sale. They answer every objection instantly and many times before the buyer stops speaking. In fact, I have watched sales people lower their rates because they could not be quiet.

'My price is $10K (1 millisecond of silence) but I can do it for less.'

NO! NO! NO! Say your price and then be quiet. It's not just sales people. In meeting after meeting I have watched my lone female clients sit in silence for the entire meeting and then perk up to volunteer for crap jobs. Why?

One woman told me "Because all the guys looked at me and expected me to do it." What?! When I checked out the recording of the meeting no one looked at her at all. She perceived that this was her job, so she decided that she had to do it. She was making herself a martyr.

Well, it is time to climb down off the cross and only volunteer for those items that we truly want to do or that can give us a leg up. It may sound a little self-serving but, if you are not serving yourself and your maid and butler are out; then who will?

Take Action

Don't let your mouth write a check that your @$$ can't cash. Before volunteering for anything, determine if the opportunity is right for you. During your next meeting as assignments are being discussed don't be the first to push your hands towards the sky and yell "PICK ME! PICK ME!" like some 'roided up 6 year old.

First ask yourself: Is this an opportunity that will fit into my schedule? Will this opportunity expose me to people that will see me at my best?

Can this opportunity be leveraged for future growth?

The next thing that you want to do is combat the verbal vomit. This can be used as a strong sales technique.

Wait 6 seconds after a customer has said their last words or before responding to anything. Collect your thoughts and then respond. If all else fails, put a lollipop in your mouth.

This is a powerful technique that can be used in sales, business, and even relationships.

Week In Review

My greatest challenge this week was:

_____

_____

_____

_____

My greatest success this week was:

_____

_____

_____

_____

I was most challenged when:

_____

_____

_____

_____

I am most proud of:

_____

_____

_____

_____

Week 28: Fear

Fear

I had only been speaking for about a year when the call came in. "Hi Dawnna. This is Monica Price and I have seen you speak at several events. I think you are amazing and would love for you to bring your expertise to my national convention in Las Vegas."

After discussing the details, I was very interested and excited to speak to Monica's group. Her organization was amazing and they had worked hard to break the mold of offerings in the conference industry. "Dawnna, I want that highly engaging style that you bring to the table along with those large group activities. No one dares to do that. Do you think you can bring that to bear for over 3000 women during an hour and a half keynote?" Monica asked.

I paused for a really, really long time. I had spoken to groups of 50 to 500 for 45 minutes; but Monica was breaking the 4 figure barrier and the 60 minute barrier.

On top of that she wanted me to do a large group activity with 3000 people. I took a deep breath and said, "Of course. Let's work out the logistics and I will create something new."

I turned to my closest confidants for support, planned every logistical element of a 3000 person activity, and prepared for nine months to ensure that this speech would be flawless. An hour before the event, I sat back stage and I was scared. Most speakers may not admit that; but I will tell you that I was really nervous. I used that nervous energy to deliver an amazing performance.

It wasn't until Monica said that the ratings were 99.875%; the highest that any speaker had ever scored; and when she hired me for next year's conference on the spot that I knew I hit the mark.

Because of that event, my career took off. Since then I have been speaking to larger and larger audiences; and I am glad to say that I am a little scared every time.

Take Action

Imagine where my career would have been had I not looked into the abyss and faced my fear. This week I want you to consider something that is well over your head and really think about how you can reach it.

Step 1: What would be bigger than you think you can handle? What would be over your head?

Step 2: Who can support you as you go for it anyway?

Step 3: How can you break down that large and scary fear into something more manageable?

Step 4: Go For It!

Step 5: How did you do? Could you do it again? What were the results?

Week In Review

My greatest challenge this week was:

_____

_____

_____

_____

_____

My greatest success this week was:

_____

_____

_____

_____

_____

I was most challenged when:

_____

_____

_____

_____

_____

I am most proud of:

_____

_____

_____

_____

_____

Week 29: Position

Position

The most common and most dreaded question asked at a networking event is "What do you do?" The person asking recognizes the protocol but worries that the response will take an hour. The person responding is terrified that they will be unclear and sound like a greasy used car salesman or go on for too long.

Let's fix this quick. My good friend Lois Creamer of "Book More Business" says that your unique selling proposition should be the first thing that falls from your lips and should only take about 6 seconds. The goal is to use an economy of words while getting to the point.

She uses a very simple format:

I work with <name of business or target market> that want to <have this result> <by taking these actions>.

For example: Lois would say, "I work with Professional Speakers that want to book more business, make more money, and reduce costly errors."

That statement is simple, direct, and to the point.

Take Action

You only have a few valuable seconds to really get someone's attention. At a networking event you want hit a home run by being specific and interesting.

Fill in the following and then repeat it for 24 hours:
I work with <name of business or target market>
that want to <have this 1-3 results>
<by taking these 1-3 actions>.

If it doesn't sound right then head back to the drawing board and revamp it.

Create several statements based on the group or target market. At your next networking event this simple statement could be your key to success.

Week In Review

My greatest challenge this week was:

_____

_____

_____

_____

_____

My greatest success this week was:

_____

_____

_____

_____

_____

I was most challenged when:

_____

_____

_____

_____

_____

I am most proud of:

_____

_____

_____

_____

_____

YOLO

Week 30: Finish

Finish

As I sat down to write another chapter in my previous book, YOLO, my husband walked in the room and said "Well, are you going to finish this project". His voice was filled with cautious doubt. That's right. Not optimism; doubt. "What in the heck is that supposed to mean?" I strongly questioned.

He pointed to the bookcase in my office that was filled with started manuscripts, half completed projects, great ideas, and to-do lists that weren't done.

He said "This bookcase is contains valuable works of incomplete brilliance. I would love to see something done."

He was right; but don't tell him I said that.

Why was it so difficult for me to complete a project that relied on just me? I could not blame someone else for not delivering or causing blockage or keeping my progress from moving forward. All of those projects were my projects that were dependent on one person; ME!

I started to notice a pattern of behavior that really impacted my forward movement. LONG To-Do-Lists.

These lists caused a serious lack of focus, required every task to be completed to perfection, and frustrated me that I could not get all 100 items on the to-do list done in one day. I am not saying that to-do lists are all bad; however, to-do lists can cause us to strive for perfection instead of completion.

When I dumped the lists YOLO was done on time and on budget!

Take Action

Instead of writing down every single task that has to be done to perfection focus on only the Top 3 important actions for the week. For example: When writing this book I wrote "write one act with a title, story, and action per week." Notice that I did not write editing, pictures, layout, publishing, etc.

Understand that one can be Perfect or Profitable. Keep in mind that technology moves forward fast without perfection and we still buy incessantly (See Apple iPhone lines). Know that you can usually create versions, volumes, and updates without cause for panic. Pick perfect or profitable.

By focusing on the Top 3 items and working towards great timely work instead of perfection the lion's share of priorities are off your plate first and you will feel more successful.

Week In Review

My greatest challenge this week was:

_____

_____

_____

_____

_____

My greatest success this week was:

_____

_____

_____

_____

_____

I was most challenged when:

_____

_____

_____

_____

_____

_____

I am most proud of:

_____

_____

_____

_____

_____

_____

Week 31: Diva

Diva

Christian Louboutin shoes, a Chado Rucci dress, and a Dior purse will not make you a Diva. Relishing the failures of other will not lift you higher and neither will treating the waitress like crap or screaming like a brat if you don't get your way.

Divas are talented, savvy, and smart women that take a bite out of life, enjoy the desserts of their hard work, and don't fret about the calories after every little nibble.

Divas are celebrated for their outstanding talent, strength, and ability to move the world around them. They simply work smart, play hard, and live among the elite.

Divas also demand and deliver nothing less than the best while keeping their ego in check. They are not uplifted by the weaknesses of others; but instead enjoy the successes of their inner circle.

Divas empower those closest to them while remaining a beacon of strength. To be clear; a diva is definitely a very strong woman; however, strong women are not always divas. While a strong woman may decide to push through a noisy night in a hotel room; a Diva will demand a correction.

So, what's the difference?

A strong woman accepts what is given, carries the weight, and pushes as hard as she can to find success; while a Diva demands what she needs to perform at the top of her game and works smarter; not harder. Although a Diva is strong, she refuses to waste her time dealing with other's misgivings, short comings, and failures that could impact her success or the success of her team.

A Diva leverages her strengths and remains honest about her own mistakes, accepts praise without letting it go to her head, and empowers others to perform above the bar... consistently.

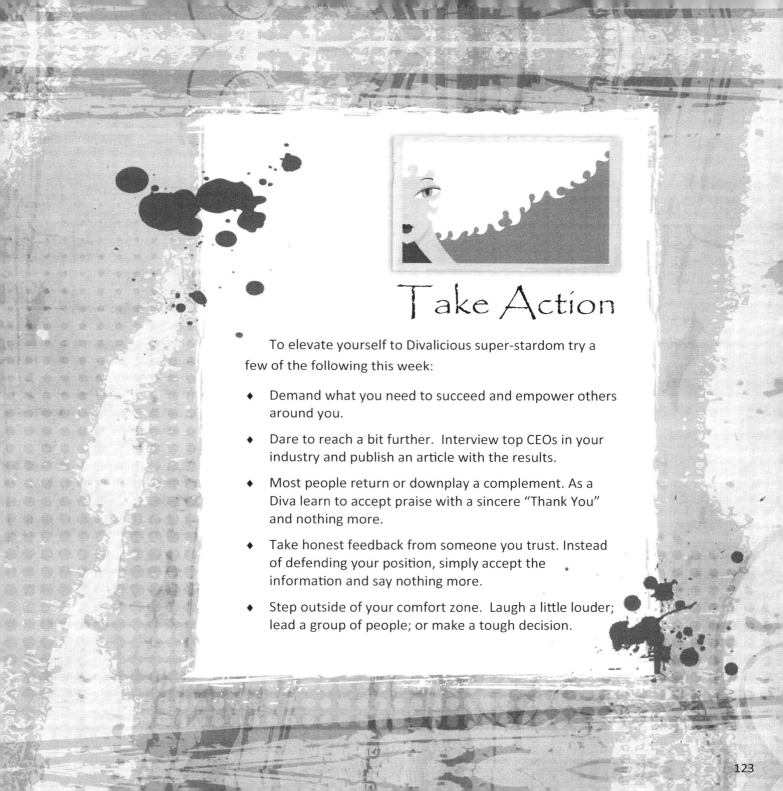

Take Action

To elevate yourself to Divalicious super-stardom try a few of the following this week:

♦ Demand what you need to succeed and empower others around you.

♦ Dare to reach a bit further. Interview top CEOs in your industry and publish an article with the results.

♦ Most people return or downplay a complement. As a Diva learn to accept praise with a sincere "Thank You" and nothing more.

♦ Take honest feedback from someone you trust. Instead of defending your position, simply accept the information and say nothing more.

♦ Step outside of your comfort zone. Laugh a little louder; lead a group of people; or make a tough decision.

Week In Review

My greatest challenge this week was:

_____

_____

_____

_____

_____

My greatest success this week was:

_____

_____

_____

_____

_____

I was most challenged when:

_____

_____

_____

_____

_____

_____

I am most proud of:

_____

_____

_____

_____

_____

_____

Week 32: Absolutely

Absolutely

Have you ever heard those positively positive people say "Anything is possible!" sounding like a 1950's TV mom with the biggest smile in the world?

"You want to be a rock-star at 85? Sure. Anything is possible! You want to eat 'Smores every day and lose weight? Why Not? Anything is possible! You want to dive head first from the 85th floor and live to tell about it? Of course you can. Because anything is possible?"

I am going to tell you a secret. Possibilities are endless; making them worthless. Probabilities, however, are much more valuable. They measure the chance that something will happen. A probability can be "nope not gonna happen" to "absolutely".

The chances of a possibility turning into a probability and becoming an occurrence are based on you getting off your @$$ and actually making something happen.

When I started speaking, I was told by speakers everywhere that it would take me years to start making money; and my chances were quite low (or improbable) that I would earn a great income.

One icon in the industry said "Of course everything is possible; but it is unlikely that it will happen for you."

"What was wrong with me?"

Her lack of belief turned into my personal fuel. Her possibility became my probability. That probability became actualized when I started earning in the mid-six figures by my second year in the industry.

Take Action

Recognize that you can do anything that you really want to. The issue is that NO ONE ever tells you how to do it. The power of realization is in the mind. Here are three steps to follow this week:

1. Determine what you want. Be specific. *For example: I want a new home; I want a new car; I want to be on stage;*

2. Design your desire. *Walk through the exact model of the home that you want. Go test drive the exact car in the exact color that you want. Go to an event where there is a stage and get on it. Ask if you can take a picture before or after an event on the stage.*

3. Create a mental image of your desire and remember how it felt to experience it (step 2).

4. Take positive action (never dwell on the negative) on your desire and know that you will get it.

5. Gratitude. *Acknowledge what you have and be thankful for it. Write a page per day of what you have and focus on the image of what you desire.*

Week In Review

My greatest challenge this week was:

_____

_____

_____

_____

_____

My greatest success this week was:

_____

_____

_____

_____

_____

I was most challenged when:

_____

_____

_____

_____

_____

I am most proud of:

_____

_____

_____

_____

_____

Week 33: Reach

Reach

Julius' goal is to always tell people that they can do better. It annoys some that he decides to be the "Master of Better".

Before their mother died Gabby and Julius promised her that the two would meet for lunch every month. Although lunch had just started, Julius had already plucked Gabby's last nerve.

Julius asked Gabby, in the most condescending manner possible, "Gabby, do you think you are living up to your full potential?" This question only came after he took a moment to consume her appearance from toes to her teeth. Julius paused as he looked at her nurses shoes and sighed when he made it to her ponytail that wasn't quite up to his standards.

Gabby knew that Julius was heading down the path of righteousness and really wanted to cut him off at the pass. She responded with, "Well Julius; do you think you are living up to yours?"

He looked her squarely in the eyes and smugly replied, "Absolutely! After all look at how much I have accomplished for myself. Who wouldn't be impressed? Of course I have reached my full potential. That is why I know so much."

Gabby noted that there was no chuckle. "This man is serious," she thought.

Since she was already annoyed at his "Master of Better" attitude and left the house without turning on the filter from her brain to her lips her response was a bit more biting than normal; "Really? This is it? This is as good as it gets? I can't expect that much more from you? Wow!"

She continued, "Julius I don't think I am living up to my full potential. In fact I think I have a lot more to learn and to do. You know when a star reaches its potential it dies. So although I am shining brightly, I know I have a lot more shining to do. You, on the other hand Julius, are growing dim and don't have much longer to live. I will try not to wear eye-popping pink to your funeral."

Take Action

Take a close look at your accomplishments this week and what you still wish to accomplish.

If you have accomplished a lot then share your accomplishments through mentoring, masterminds, and volunteerism. Sharing will keep your star looking radiant.

If you are working and learning new things, then put them into action at work, volunteerism, and masterminds. You can also find a mentor that will help you get this part of your star shining a little brighter.

Remember, you want to reach for your potential and share it so that you can continue to grow.

Week In Review

My greatest challenge this week was:

_____
_____
_____
_____
_____

My greatest success this week was:

_____
_____
_____
_____
_____

I was most challenged when:

_____
_____
_____
_____
_____
_____
_____

I am most proud of:

_____
_____
_____
_____
_____
_____
_____

Week 34: Promoted

Promoted

Sometimes on the way up the corporate ladder, the rungs can get a little slippery and you can quickly find yourself sliding in the wrong direction or just holding on for dear life.

You might look around and wonder how did she get that promotion; why is he in a new department; or why did they go with someone from the outside.

It is easy to get so caught up in the day to day consumption of a full plate of work that we ignore the dessert tray of opportunities that are passing us by.

When I was working as a Technical Educator, I figured out quickly that were ways to get noticed beyond my work in the classroom. In fact, figuring out how to get noticed afforded me several opportunities. I learned what my talents were, how I could leverage those talents beyond my day-to-day work, and then further use those talents to promote myself.

Besides being offered a Director Level role, I was also asked to present to a congressional committee in order to requisition funds for a Federal Courthouse. By delivering this presentation, stepping outside of my comfort zone, and leveraging my talent I found myself on the path toward my future success.

This simple secret was the first step towards living out my true passion as I climbed the corporate ladder.

Take Action

It's time to make that move in three simple steps.

First: There is something that your boss struggles with, hates doing, or wants to get off of her plate. It could be a monthly report, a regular meeting, or dealing with a resource. Your job is to find out what that is.

Next: Jump ahead and get the work done that your boss hates to do. The trick is that you have to get it done before they start working on it; you have to make sure that it is correct; and you have to know the information perfectly. This gives you credibility. Don't expect a promotion after doing this one time. You have to deliver consistently. Another trick is to solve an issue and offer to manage the implementation of the solution. Notice that I did not say execute the solution.

Finally: Shamelessly Self Promote your work (see Shameless) and make sure that your boss or the powers that be are aware of your leadership skills and successes. Let it be known that you are interested in offering more value to your organization.

Week In Review

My greatest challenge this week was:

_____

_____

_____

_____

_____

I was most challenged when:

_____

_____

_____

_____

_____

My greatest success this week was:

_____

_____

_____

_____

_____

I am most proud of:

_____

_____

_____

_____

_____

Week 35: Spite

Spite

As Lisa Schwartz, a Mary Kay Director, stared at her reflection in the mirror she made a decision, "Mediocrity is a poor bedfellow and I am better than this." After being a part of the Mary Kay organization for 7 years she knew that she could be better, do better, and deserved better.

With a father in his final stages of cancer and a mother in treatment for breast cancer, Lisa had several reasons to be lax, but instead promised her father that she could take care of herself once he was gone. To prove it she would earn an elusive limited edition Mary Kay Mustang. This meant that she had to triple her efforts quickly.

Lisa created three milestones to reach her goal: complete the "100 Face Challenge", recruit and mentor women on her team, and develop her own organization. After the New Year's festivities were over Lisa got to work.

"I had no idea how I would find 100 women to complete the challenge and by the third week of January my monthly quota seemed like a pipe dream; but I kept my eye on the goal and within five days I earned 150% of my quota. Over the next three months I completed the 100 Faces Challenge and developed a team of top performers. But my life was falling apart. My father was in hospice, my mother had undergone surgery, and life was throwing roadblocks that made my promise seem impossible. "

"My motivation was at an all-time low, but it was my responsibility to keep my business on track and my promise to my dad," said Lisa.

Although Lisa refocused her efforts and was moving full steam ahead the next devastating blow could have easily derailed her. "When my dad passed away on June 15th, I was crushed under the weight of heartbreak. I had no idea where the strength would come from to work through funeral arrangements, finalize his estate, care for my mother, and heal the hole in my heart. Everyone said that I should give up on the goal, after all he was gone. I kept thinking 'I made my dad a promise; I have 15 days to keep it'."

On June 30th, her father's birthday, Lisa earned the Limited Edition Mary Kay Mustang. "I knew there were perfectly placed mountains, craters, and obstacles on my path, but my dad gave me the strength to persevere and move forward in spite of it all. My father taught me to never use life as an excuse to give up. So I used my bond with him to succeed."

When Lisa finally grieved her dad's loss she felt like there was room to give that process the proper reverence it deserved. .

Take Action

Lisa's perseverance in spite of everything that was going on in her life was amazing. I felt like I had no excuses for failure. During our conversation she made it clear that she did three things consistently:

Put the bar a little higher than you can reach and never stop reaching for it.

Create an outcome (or goal) with a few milestones. Don't try to know all the steps to each milestone and each goal. When you complete a step that works, then take another step. If that step does not work rethink your actions and try again.

Recognize that you are making choices every day to move forward or not. I made a choice to grieve my father's loss after I reached the goal; I made a choice to keep a promise.

Failure was an option but, I chose a different direction.

Week In Review

My greatest challenge this week was:

_____

_____

_____

_____

_____

My greatest success this week was:

_____

_____

_____

_____

_____

I was most challenged when:

_____

_____

_____

_____

_____

I am most proud of:

_____

_____

_____

_____

_____

Week 36: Partnerships

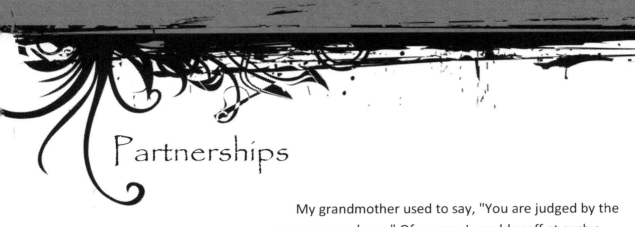

Partnerships

My grandmother used to say, "You are judged by the company you keep." Of course, I would scoff at such a ridiculous saying which only seemed to pop up when she was judging (rightfully so) the selection of one of my friends. Now I recognize that she was telling me that I needed to have a stronger network that I could leverage if I plan to succeed in life.

She was right. Great partnerships are an awesome way to boost your business or your value to those around you. Leveraging those partnerships appropriately gives you higher likability and your network feels like they know you better based on them

There is a caveat. Just like my grandmother said that I was judged by my company, you will also be judged by your network. A weak network of resources that are not available, lack accuracy, have poor partners and are not a resource of information will reflect poorly on you.

Take Action

This week take a closer look at you and your network. Most of us network in groups containing people with same expertise. This is great for learning and mentoring, but not for complementing skills or correcting areas of deficit. We want to have a well-rounded network that allows us to create and leverage partnerships.

- What are your areas of expertise? Use these skills to be known as the expert.

- What are your areas of deficit? Find people that are reliable experts in these areas and fill your network with them.

- What networks can use your skills? Take a look at the areas where you are the weakest; join networks of professionals that have these skills.

Week In Review

My greatest challenge this week was:

_____

_____

_____

_____

_____

My greatest success this week was:

_____

_____

_____

_____

_____

I was most challenged when:

_____

_____

_____

_____

_____

I am most proud of:

_____

_____

_____

_____

_____

Week 37: Shameless

Shameless

You have probably heard the saying "If you don't toot your own horn then no one else will." That saying has never been truer or more relevant than right now, in this challenging economic climate and competitive business environment.

Michelle Villalobos, creator of the Shameless Self-Promotion keynote & workshop series on Personal Branding, says, "When you look at all the premium brands out there - from organic rice, to expensive cars, to designer jeans, to luxury hotels and everything in between, notice that the ones with the highest perceived value are able to attract business and charge more. If you as an individual want to EARN more, then it's crucial that you understand that YOU are a brand too, and like it or not, your brand determines your market value. The key to building a great personal brand is to undertake a strategic effort to raise your perceived value – without turning people off. Women often struggle with this balancing act because we're taught to be modest and humble; we've been socialized to see self-promotion as 'braggy,' which is 'unfeminine.' Those who master the art of Shameless – never shameFUL – Self-Promotion in a way that's authentic, compelling and appealing, will attract more high-profile opportunities and earn more money. Period."

So start promoting yourself! Be bold and proud of your accomplishments. While you definitely don't want to go overboard "Donald-Trump-style," it is essential that you somehow let others know how awesome you are, what you have accomplished, and the immense value you contribute. This is truly one of the characteristics of Audacious Women.

Take Action

This week is all about gracefully tooting your own horn and sound great doing it. There are three simple steps.

Identify the issue or need and make sure that you separate yourself from the issue. Next: State how you created or helped to create a solution. Finally: Talk about the results as a benefit and who benefited from the results.

Here is an example:

(The issue) ABWA needed a professional speaker for their national conference. They were struggling to find the right fit.

(The Solution) I knew of a woman that was a fantastic mix of Tony Robbins Motivational Style with a splash of Blue Man Group whole audience experience with a nice dose of Steve Jobs business acumen thrown in. I booked Dawnna within 72 hours and the problem was solved.

(The Result) Not only did she do a fantastic job that kept our audience completely engaged; she also came early, stayed late; and answered questions for all three days of the event.

Week In Review

My greatest challenge this week was:

_____

_____

_____

_____

_____

My greatest success this week was:

_____

_____

_____

_____

I was most challenged when:

_____

_____

_____

_____

_____

_____

I am most proud of:

_____

_____

_____

_____

_____

_____

Week 38: Let Go

Let Go

What sets you off? I mean that thing that really sets your panties on fire and makes you spew all kinds of nastiness.

My good friend Gibby will tell you that it is bad driving. Gibby is a very good and very defensive driver. One morning on our way to a business meeting someone in the left lane on the highway decided that they needed to make a right turn.

Gibby went from having a great conversation filled with laughter to a road raging maniac that wanted to track down someone that had obviously gotten their driver's license from a Cracker Jack box.

She talked about it during the remainder of our 65 minute drive; she told everyone at the conference; she talked about it on the way home; and made reference to the incident during our conversation three days later. Gibby could not let go.

Conversely, I have been in the car with Cathy who is a "stereotypical bad driver".

She pays little attention to signs, pauses in the middle of traffic to find parking, and generally considers driving a secondary action to figuring out where she is going or what she is looking for. Cathy never frets or worries when she drives and is probably the person that drives Gibby insane!

If someone does offend Cathy she turns the incident into a joke by creating an outrageous excuse about their behavior.

Someone speeding has to "Get home and drop a deuce"; someone turning the wrong way "never learned their left from their right" or "they are from another country"; someone that is angry "has a mother that never loved him because he was a bed wetter until he was 22 years old".

Cathy goes on to make up a full story about this total stranger and their issues until everyone in the car has a full belly laugh (regardless of how terrified we are from her driving).

The point is that Cathy can let go and move on while Gibby stresses the point until it stresses her out.

Take Action

We can only control what we can control. Everything else... we have to let go.

This week is a time to analyze what you can and can't control. So many times we are offended by others that have no clue that they have actually offended us. And while they drive along like Cathy, we are stressed out about the situation like Gibby.

Honestly, Cathy is the happiest person that I know and Gibby was taking blood pressure meds before she was 30.

Take a close look at those things that bother you. If they are in your control then change them. If they are not then create an outrageous excuse for the behavior; visualize that excuse as being true; have a personal chuckle; and then let go.

Now enjoy a week filled with more laughs.

Week In Review

My greatest challenge this week was:

_____

_____

_____

_____

_____

My greatest success this week was:

_____

_____

_____

_____

_____

I was most challenged when:

_____

_____

_____

_____

_____

I am most proud of:

_____

_____

_____

_____

_____

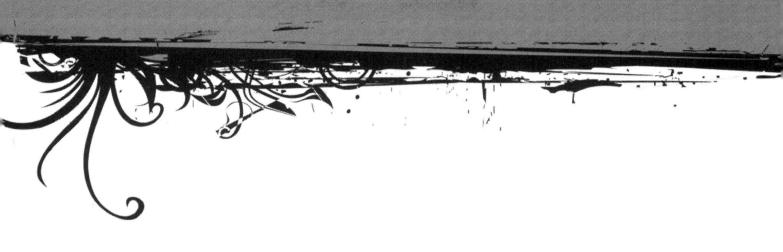

Week of

Reflection

Audacious women recognize that there is a huge difference between responsibility and blame.

Blame is the quicksand that leads to finger-pointing and fault-finding with no opportunity for correction or reflection.

Responsibility, when applied appropriately, is the mirror that lets us reflect on our actions, learn valuable lessons, and make the steps on our path with a higher level of knowledge.

Audacious women are smart enough to recognize the quicksand of blame and instead step on the pathway that leads to a higher ground.

Reflection

What have you learned about yourself?

_____

_____

_____

_____

I have shared my new knowledge with:

_____

_____

_____

_____

The toughest action was:

_____

_____

_____

_____

The week that I will retry is:

_____

_____

_____

_____

Reflection

My biggest accomplishment was:

_____

_____

_____

_____

_____

What surprised me about myself was:

_____

_____

_____

_____

I am the proudest of myself because:

_____

_____

_____

_____

_____

What I plan to do differently is:

_____

_____

_____

_____

_____

Week 40: Evangelist

Evangelist

My close friend, Tracy, had been trying to close a customer for six months. "We've had dinner; we've gone to lunch; I have wooed her beyond the limits of WOOING!", said Tracy.

But when she got into the details, Tracy wasn't wooing; she was evangelizing! Instead of sharing the results of working with her; Tracy was telling her prospect HOW she was going to make it to the mountain top and convert dimes into dollars.

You have doused your prospect in the holy water of your process; and evangelized about every step you take and they still won't convert to a customer. Well, surprise, surprise; there is no money in being an Evangelist; at least not to the "un-converted".

Think about it this way: Do you care how your local grocer gets the fruit from the field to the store or do you care that you will have fresh, sweet, and ripe fruit available when you want it? Most people care about the latter.

Many people spend loads of time talking about the process and not the results. Many customers want to know the results and not the process. In fact, when a prospect gets too deep into the process they are likely looking for a way to exclude you.

It is time to get down from the pulpit and really talk about the results of working with you so that people will want to... work with you.

Take Action

You are going to talk about the results of your work instead of how you do your work.

1. What do you do? What is your expertise? Ex: Certified Project Manager.

2. How do you deliver your expertise? Ex: I follow the PMI's methods for moving a project forward by managing scope, schedule, and cost.

3. What are the results? Ex: Quality products; On time; Reduced risk of failure; Saved money; Higher ROI.

4. What do you do differently? What is your specialty? Ex: I specialize in correcting distressed projects.

5. Who is your target market. Ex: Not for Profits.

When someone asks you what you do, you can say: "I work with Not-For-Profits to save money by delivering quality products on time and within budget. As a Certified Project Manager, I specialize in significantly reducing the risk of failure for distressed projects."

*PMI- Certifying body for Project Managers

Week In Review

My greatest challenge this week was:

_____

_____

_____

_____

_____

My greatest success this week was:

_____

_____

_____

_____

_____

I was most challenged when:

_____

_____

_____

_____

_____

I am most proud of:

_____

_____

_____

_____

_____

Week 41: Build First

Build

Sasha is so full of ideas that spark stories for speeches, books, and life lessons that lead me to share more with the world. But muse is only one part of her life; she also has a business. As an idea person Sasha easily sees solutions to problems and how quickly they can be solved. Her gift is also her struggle.

As easily as she can come up with an idea; Sasha may also underestimate its implementation and full life-cycle. Because her excitement is so contagious, Sasha can usually convince others that implementation is a cake walk.

Her vernacular is filled with phrases such as "This is really straight-forward and simple, so much so, that we can get this up and running pretty quickly" and "If I build it they will come" and "Everyone will buy this amazing idea yesterday?"

One weekend Sasha started development on three different ideas but did not focus on any single one.

By the time week four came around she was struggling to complete her regular work plus the work of completing the three new projects that Sasha had taken on. Her team was a little frustrated and wanted to have a single focus towards success.

Sasha's story is no different from many women in business or business in general. According to the Standish group 87% of all projects started fail due to incomplete scope. Basically the work was underestimated although the idea seemed pretty good at the time.

How many great ideas do you start and don't complete? How many of those ideas seem sweet at first but give you a toothache at the end?

The old adage is that if you build it they will come. The Audacious Woman will tell you, don't build it until you have sold enough to cover the costs and make a little profit to boot.

Take Action

All ideas seem great at first. They usually happen when our inhibitions are low and our endorphins are high. Meaning that ideas feel good. The sweet taste of an idea can cause a toothache in the end. Although we will strike while the iron is hot our goal is not to get burnt.

In order to keep you out of idea implementation hell, simply follow a few rules of thumb to help you determine if an idea is really a good idea.

#1: Before implementing think about it for 30 days. You should still be in love or start to question its implementation within a month.

#2: Think of implementation in terms of work, schedule, cost, quality, human resources, communications, risk, and procurement. Then sales, implementation, and support.

#3: Break down your idea into phases. What would you want to do first (must have) and what could you add on later?

#4: Finally, before you do anything. Sell the idea. If it is a book, get pre-orders. If you can't sell it, it may not be cooked enough just yet.

Week In Review

My greatest challenge this week was:

_____

_____

_____

_____

_____

My greatest success this week was:

_____

_____

_____

_____

_____

I was most challenged when:

_____

_____

_____

_____

_____

I am most proud of:

_____

_____

_____

_____

_____

Week 42: Tempt

Tempt

At around eight years old, most little boys decide that they will get their first kiss. Regardless of whether it is a peck on the cheek or forehead, they are looking for someone other than mom and grandma to make this happen.

Derek Brown asked me for a kiss. I was seven and he was the older man at eight years old. My answer was absolutely not! Derek then asked Georgia, April, and Karen. Every time Derek asked and got rejected he reviewed his game plan, made changes, and tried again. Karen gave up the kiss.

Fast forward 10 years to the Sadie Hawkins dance where girls ask boys to the dance. At 17 years old I asked (you guessed it) Derek Brown who said absolutely not. I ran home cracked open some Chunky Monkey ice cream and called my friend Lisa to talk about the crushing blow to my ego.

We discussed all of the things that were wrong with me; my hair, my clothes, my body; my teeth; my shoe size, etc.

Amazing! Rejection to us means that we are flawed; and to men it means regroup and try again from another angle.

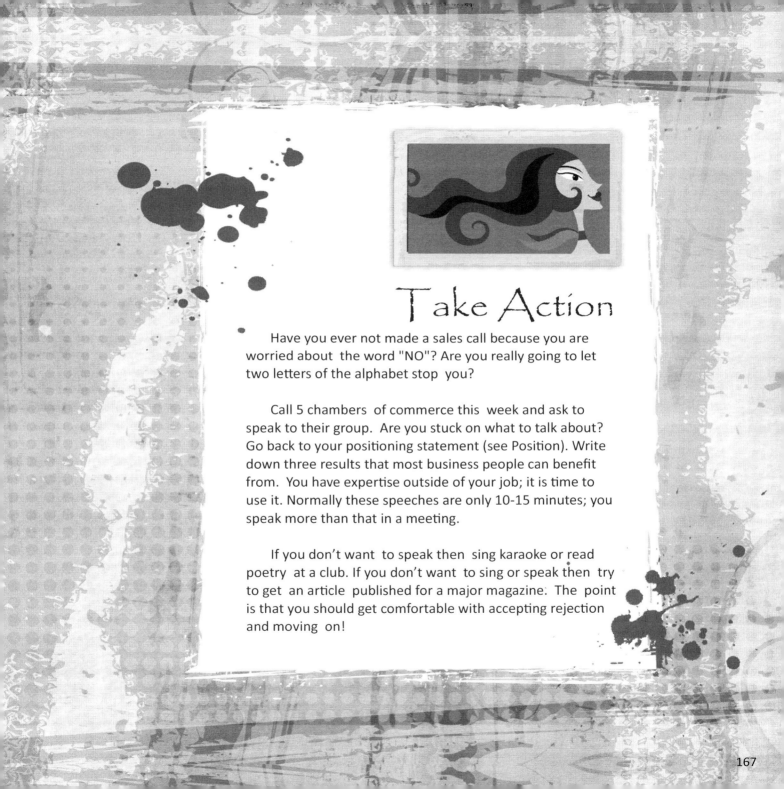

Take Action

Have you ever not made a sales call because you are worried about the word "NO"? Are you really going to let two letters of the alphabet stop you?

Call 5 chambers of commerce this week and ask to speak to their group. Are you stuck on what to talk about? Go back to your positioning statement (see Position). Write down three results that most business people can benefit from. You have expertise outside of your job; it is time to use it. Normally these speeches are only 10-15 minutes; you speak more than that in a meeting.

If you don't want to speak then sing karaoke or read poetry at a club. If you don't want to sing or speak then try to get an article published for a major magazine. The point is that you should get comfortable with accepting rejection and moving on!

Week In Review

My greatest challenge this week was:

_____
_____
_____
_____
_____

My greatest success this week was:

_____
_____
_____
_____
_____

I was most challenged when:

_____
_____
_____
_____
_____
_____

I am most proud of:

_____
_____
_____
_____
_____
_____

Week 43: Praise

Praise

My son Tray has always been really smart; sometimes a little too smart. He was the kid that snuck a screwdriver into his bedroom and started taking apart every toy that he owned when he was three. When I walked in a mini piano, remote controlled car, and xylophone all became victims to his curiosity.

Once Tray started school he did not really understand the value of grades until the third grade.

On this particular afternoon, now in the 7th grade, Tray proudly walked in and handed me his science grade; a class that he had been struggling in until he realized that they could dissect frogs. Tray was still excited about finding out how things worked... even frogs (eeeewww)

Tray's teacher did not just send the end grade she let the parents know all of the grades that led up to the end grade.

As I scanned the sheet, I glanced over the multitude of A's, eyed a few B's, paused at some C's and came to a complete halt when I saw an F. "What is this Tray? Why do you have an F on here?" I scorned, "You know what, go to your room."

A few minutes later Tray's brother walked in and saw the paper and said "WOW! Tray got an A in science? That is so cool. I knew he liked dissecting frogs and worms."

I was so fixed on the bad stuff that I never noticed the end result. He moved his grade up from a D to an A in one quarter. The F on the list was for...well actually... it does not matter because the outcome would still have been an A.

He delivered a fantastic result. I taught them that they can be perfect or profitable. Tray, in this case, was profitable and I was a hypocrite seeking perfection.

Take Action

The rest of the story: I apologized to Tray and explained that sometimes even mommies lose sight of the goal. I don't think it mattered much because he passed out after the apology. When he woke up he said that he dreamed that he caught a unicorn or that a woman admitted she was wrong. Did I mention he was a smart ass?

Audacious Women check the details of delivery but don't let the minor pebbles on the path stop them from walking it in stilettos and reaching the goal. They also don't yell until the pebbles are removed or for there being pebbles on the path; they just keep walking.

Take a look at the little things and correct where you can; but first ask yourself will it impact how you reach the goal. If it doesn't then don't sweat it.

Sometimes, you can't sweat the small stuff.

Week In Review

My greatest challenge this week was:

_____

_____

_____

_____

_____

My greatest success this week was:

_____

_____

_____

_____

_____

I was most challenged when:

_____

_____

_____

_____

_____

I am most proud of:

_____

_____

_____

_____

_____

Week 44: Trust

Trust

Women's intuition, instinct, or spidy senses; whatever you call it, there is a sixth sense that constantly leads us in the right direction and many times it is ignored; usually for fear that it is not well thought out.

It is the ability to acquire knowledge without inference and/or the use of reason. Intuition happens in a blink. It is the powerful yet fleeting moment that compels you to do something. You will hear people talk about how they felt it in their gut. The biggest impedance to intuition is our own over analysis and lack of self-belief.

Audaciously Successful women follow their gut regardless of what "the numbers" may have dictated. The consistent mantra of an Audacious Woman is "If I can't trust myself then why should anyone else?"

Intuition in Action

"The hairs on the back of my neck were at full attention. At that very moment I moved out of the way right before that car was about to hit me" Janet R - Fairfax, VA

"Something told me that I should go. I felt pressed to be there. Who would have guessed that I would strike the deal of a lifetime." Oprah Winfrey

"I had a feeling that I should call her. She said 'OMG! I was just sitting here feeling like I needed to talk to you'" - Countless numbers of women

"I knew my baby needed me." Even more women. "My gut told me that there was more to it so I kept investigating even though the case was closed." - Police Detectives around the world

Take Action

This week is all about the decisions that happen in a blink. Don't worry we won't be asking you to guess what the next card is in the deck; this is not about clairvoyance; it's about trusting your gut.

Take every opportunity to make instant decisions this week regardless of how insignificant or important.

For example: If someone asks you "What do you want for lunch" say the first thing that you feel. Notice that I did not say "Think of". Might seem slight; but feelings happen in an instant and thoughts follow. This week you are going to follow that first feeling that happens in a blink.

If you feel like calling someone, then call them. If you feel like going somewhere, don't let the couch suck you in; GO! If you feel like you should speak to a perfect stranger, say hello. Don't get me wrong; I am not saying if you feel like eating a tub of Chubby Hubby Ice Cream then do so. That is a craving that will have lasting effects in all the wrong areas. I am saying to trust your gut and see where it leads you. I have a feeling that you will be pleasantly surprised.

Week In Review

My greatest challenge this week was:

_____

_____

_____

_____

_____

My greatest success this week was:

_____

_____

_____

_____

I was most challenged when:

_____

_____

_____

_____

_____

I am most proud of:

_____

_____

_____

_____

_____

Week 45: Cha-Ching

Cha-Ching

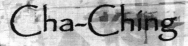

Sometimes people call me lucky because I moved up the ladder so quickly from CSR to C-Level Exec of a Tech company in 15 years. They also think I am lucky because I am called on by organizations around the world as a Premier Speaker and Expert. I don't think luck has anything to do with it.

In my opinion, it is not only being in the right place at the right time; but doing something extraordinary when you arrive. I knew it wasn't my high powered education; I did not get a BS in Information Technology until I retired from the corporate world at 40. And it wasn't my High-Powered contacts; I actually lived in my car when I was 19.

The first thing I knew was that I deserved more than living in a car. From that point, I did everything I could to increase my perceived value. The most important thing to remember is that if you don't think that you deserve more; then there is nothing in this book that I can write to make you believe that you do.

But you are more Audacious now than you were a few weeks ago, so let's start making more cha-ching.

Take Action

Step 1: Define your current level of expertise, a level below where you are, and a level that is totally over your head. Look for opportunities at each level to validate your findings:

- *Hostage* - You can't change because your skills, pay, or expertise are no longer needed in the marketplace; Take a class or volunteer to increase your skills.

- *Undervalued* - Doing a lot more work that you are being valued for;

- *Aligned* - You are getting exactly what you deserve for what you bring to the table.

Step 2: Go for an opportunity that is below where you will agree to work. (i.e. Manager trying out as a receptionist.) If you get an offer, negotiate as if your life depended on it. Then recommend someone that would be a more appropriate fit.

Do you feel like you are wasting time? Get over it. You are mastering two critical skills. Passing on business that is not the right fit and negotiations.

Step 3: For the position that is over your head; instead of interviewing for it; attack it like a research project. You know that they are never going to hire you so find out what the upper level is all about and what you need to do to get there. Turn the tables on the interviewer and get what you need out of this opportunity.

Results: You might be surprised to find that you are offered the position that is over your head. By taking a position of power and running the interview; you show that you have great leadership skills. Now that you have an offer, leverage those negotiation skills and determine if this is an opportunity that you really want. Don't get me wrong; you have to have some knowledge and experience; but confidence, talent, and a good personality go a long way.

Optional Step: Become volunteer leader to learn how to work with and lead people that have nothing to lose.

Week In Review

My greatest challenge this week was:

_____

_____

_____

_____

_____

I was most challenged when:

_____

_____

_____

_____

_____

_____

My greatest success this week was:

_____

_____

_____

_____

_____

I am most proud of:

_____

_____

_____

_____

_____

_____

Week 46: $90k Mirror

$90K Mirror

Alexa's client wanted her to work with them to correct some serious project issues. She created a value based contract that paid her a percentage of savings based on results. This means that on her $40 million project, a savings of 10% could mean $4 million in their pocket and $100K in Alexa's.

Considering the projects estimated return on investment (ROI) was currently non-existent; any savings would be a significant upgrade, lots of people would still have their jobs including Mr. President (the person that hired her).

Within the four weeks Alexa developed a roadmap had begun implementation. Within 6 weeks she had corrected and removed most of the expense tasks. By the time they reached the 8 week mark, deliverables were rolling in and the ROI had significantly increased.

The goals were met and the company would save $4 million for the first round. Alexa was excited because she knew that payday was here!

Prior to payment Mr. President sent Alexa a note that read, "After reviewing your roadmap it seems that you gave us solutions that were right under our noses. It seems unfair to pay someone $100,000 for 4 weeks of actual work for something that we could have found ourselves".

Alexa agreed; to some it may seem ridiculous to pay someone $100,000 for four weeks of actual work. But Alexa was not getting paid for time; she was delivering results. Mr. President continued to tell her that he thought $10K was a fair amount for 4 weeks of work.

Alexa agreed and sent a new invoice and a mirror wrapped in a shiny red box. The invoice read, "Four weeks of actual work: $10K; A mirror to see what is right under your nose: $90K".

Although Mr. President laughed he got the point, paid the invoice, and wants to work with Alexa on a new project.

Take Action

Remember that time is finite and money is infinite; therefore there is no amount of money can pay for your time.

This week is all about learning your value and truly understanding where your value lies.

Mantra: Time is finite; money is infinite. This means that my time is more valuable that your project.

What results can you deliver and how can you value those results?

Week In Review

My greatest challenge this week was:

_____

_____

_____

_____

_____

My greatest success this week was:

_____

_____

_____

_____

I was most challenged when:

_____

_____

_____

_____

_____

I am most proud of:

_____

_____

_____

_____

_____

Week 47: Reliable

Reliable

Can you imagine becoming a resource that is so accurate and available with amazing partnerships that people actually use your name in replace of a common task? Thinks it's not possible; then think again. Google did just that by replacing the phrase "do a search on the internet" with "Google it".

My goal is to create a style of speaking that people call it the St Louis Style or they say that a speaker is "Dawnna-ing it". Ok, so it has a way to go but, I think you get the drift.

Google is a great example to follow. They started off doing one thing and doing it well. Google made sure that they were accurate (in fact the most accurate) in delivering search results. They followed that up with availability. They not only served up results 24 hours per day (as expected with anything online) they served them up fast. They expanded their reach by partnering with developers that could offer solutions their loyal customers desperately wanted. They also provided information to web site owners about how to get higher rankings on their search engine results. This made them a reliable resource that customers could not do without.

What do you want to be known for? Imagine your area of expertise being known as "<Your Name Here>-ing it".

Take Action

This week you are going to concentrate on how to tell your customers, partners, and prospects to do what you do. It may seem counterintuitive, but remember that they can't do what you do without you.

Write down something that you do well or that you know? Write a blog-post, e-book, audio, or video about what you do. Be bold and create a complete video series about your knowledge.

Share that information with your network and watch yourself become a reliable resource.

Week In Review

My greatest challenge this week was:

_____
_____
_____
_____
_____

I was most challenged when:

_____
_____
_____
_____
_____
_____
_____

My greatest success this week was:

_____
_____
_____
_____
_____

I am most proud of:

_____
_____
_____
_____
_____
_____
_____

Week 48: WingDiva

WingDiva

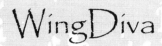

Networking can be a challenge that starts from the moment you get that invite. The questions start plaguing your mind as if obstacles to a goal.

"Is it too far? What time does it start? How much does it cost? Should I go? Who do I know? OMG! The people! That guy that grabs every business card in the room like a high-schooler collecting phone numbers just to spam you; what about the guy that tries to get you in on the ground floor of the latest MLM? Or the lady that wants to do coffee but never sets up a time.*

Finally, you give up... "Never mind! I am exhausted thinking about it. Plus, I don't want to be one of those people that sound like one of *those* people."

What you need is a wing-man (or Diva). This is someone that can introduce you to the people that are the right fit for your business, run interference, and keep you off of those funky e-mail lists.

Imagine this instead:

Janet and you are going to a networking event across town. You will meet at the local Starbucks and carpool (always fun). She works for ProjectX as a project management director. Her positioning statement is "I work with enterprise organizations that want to remove obstacles so their projects can move forward faster." She is networking to expand her current network, learn about current PM organizational challenges, and to find people to interview for an upcoming article.

Janet knows your role, positioning statement, why you're networking, and who you are looking to meet.

During the evening Janet will be on the lookout for people that would be perfect for you to meet. She will save you after a conversation has gone on for 10 minutes. And finally, Janet will carry around some of your business cards to pass out. Don't worry; you will be doing the same for her.

*They obviously did not read this book or that would never happen.

Take Action

Reflective networking is all about promoting your networking partner. Shine a spotlight on them and it will reflect back to you. Of course you will say your positioning statement (see Position); however, you are really looking to find people that are a great fit for your partner and then make an introduction. If your partner is busy, then give out their business card and make an introduction later.

Steps to Success:

First: Find a good networking partner

Second: Learn each other's positioning statement.

Third: Each of you should answer these questions: Why are you networking and who are looking to meet? Be specific. EVERYONE is the wrong answer.

Fourth: What is the signal or amount of time that you are willing to chat with someone. For example: "10 minutes" or "When I drop my napkin" or "When I throw my cellphone at your head come save me".

Week In Review

My greatest challenge this week was:

_____

_____

_____

_____

_____

I was most challenged when:

_____

_____

_____

_____

_____

_____

My greatest success this week was:

_____

_____

_____

_____

_____

I am most proud of:

_____

_____

_____

_____

_____

_____

Week 49: Magnifico

Magnifico

Magnifico the Magician is an amazing performer and wants to make his act better. He is not sure exactly what to do, but decides on the "saw a person in half" trick. He starts marketing the new and improved act in order to generate buzz. He spends days on social media and direct marketing efforts.

With this new level of risk and excitement, Magnifico decides to raise ticket prices that his target market is comfortable with.

Magnifico then starts working on sales and sponsorships. He spends days on these efforts.

Finally he realizes that he has not added the new trick into the flow of his current act. So Magnifico spends days trying to figure out the best flow of the act.

It is opening night and Magnifico realizes that he has not hired a person to saw in half; nor has he practiced. So he decides that he will "up the ante" and saw himself in half using a pendulum saw.

The pendulum saw will swing over his boxed body and then he will come out of the box put back together and amaze his crowd.

Magnifico's funeral was Friday.

Take Action

Are you killing your business by not creating a circle of knowledge, support and influence. Don't be like Magnifico, instead be magnificent. Use the quadrant below:

Quadrant 1: Enter tasks where you have low knowledge and it is a low priority then, get an expert to handle this for you.

Quadrant 2. Enter tasks where you have high knowledge, but this is a low priority, then get someone that knows more than you about the subject and can work to your high standard. This is an area of challenge. You will have to let go and trust someone else.

Quadrant 3. Enter tasks where you have low knowledge, but this area is a high priority, then get a mentor to guide you or buy coaching.

Quadrant 4. Enter tasks where you have high knowledge and this is a high priority. This is your area of expertise that you should be using to generate income.

		Knowledge	
		LOW	HIGH
Tasks	LOW	1	2
	HIGH	3	4

Week In Review

My greatest challenge this week was:

_____

_____

_____

_____

My greatest success this week was:

_____

_____

_____

_____

I was most challenged when:

_____

_____

_____

_____

_____

I am most proud of:

_____

_____

_____

_____

_____

Week 50: Risk

Risk

Since I could remember I would perform actions that other people considered risky. When I lived in my car everyone was worried about the security risk; but I knew that I was safe. When I retired from corporate life and decided to become a speaker, I was told that being on stage in front of thousands is risky. "Anything could wrong," they would say. But I knew that everything would be great because I had already experienced each activity.

Risk is the difference between taking action with prior experience and taking action without it. This might sound difficult; but with a little practice it is easier than you think.

Before I took the stage for the first time I did three things: created an outcome; developed the milestones; and immersed myself in the experience ahead of time.

I wanted to create an event that fully engaged the audience; allow them to experience information (rather than just hearing about it); and leave them with the excitement to take action. That was the outcome. Then, I created whole audience activities that allowed each person to experience the information, developed a message that infused humor and engaged audience members, and added actionable items that each attendee would be excited to do. These were my milestones.

Finally, a day before the event, I sat on the stage and looked out into the audience of empty seats. I could hear the people chuckle as I gave my speech; I watched the activities unfold; and walked through each moment of the event. I knew how to start, end, and execute before actually standing on the podium in front of 1000s of people. This was the experience that I needed.

Immersion Visualization allows you to play out different scenarios and fully prepare for any "unexpected" changes. When the unexpected is expected and experienced, the risk is reduced.

This simple yet powerful exercise helps singers, actors, and many performers prepare. By leveraging this in everyday life, I have been able to experience difficult conversations and face them with well thought out solutions; take on feats that others see as impossible or difficult; and consider "unexpected elements" to prepare for them quickly.

My events are considered "Whole Audience Experiences" because at some point, the entire audience will have the opportunity to participate in an activity (that does not include just talking to their neighbors or writing notes). At the beginning of the speech I ask audience members to visualize themselves on stage with me; to see the audience; and to hear the applause. Then I ask them to visualize how to introduce themselves and something unexpected such as a trip or an odd question or dancing.

This simple three minute activity increased participation exponentially. Instead of getting a few people to raise their hands, many people felt prepared so we would have hundreds of people ready to participate.

Now it is your turn.

Consider something you have never done but is simple to do; such as flying a kite. Fully immerse yourself in the activity and every step of it. Feel the wind on your face and the tug of the kite in the sky. Consider how you will complete lift off. What are the risks?

Are there power lines, trees, homes, etc. How will you handle those risks? How will you react if the string snaps? How will you avoid that risk or will you?

Now complete the activity and consider how you feel.

Try again with something more difficult.

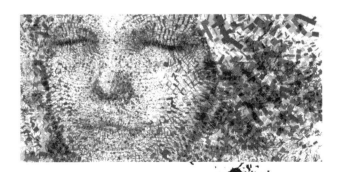

Week In Review

My greatest challenge this week was:

_____

_____

_____

_____

_____

My greatest success this week was:

_____

_____

_____

_____

_____

I was most challenged when:

_____

_____

_____

_____

_____

_____

I am most proud of:

_____

_____

_____

_____

_____

_____

Week 51: Naked

Naked

Gibby is a perfect size 6. She is a gorgeous model type Amazonian woman of 6' tall with a beautiful smile and flawless skin. People look at Gibby and think "Wow! She is gorgeous". Which is usually followed by their wishes; "I wish I were that tall; I wish I had that skin; I wish I had that body; I wish I had that smile; I wish I had that <fill in your wish>".

During a recent speaking event for the American Business Women's Association, I asked the audience filled with hundreds of women to write down 10 things about their neighbor that was beautiful from the inside out. Then I asked them to write another 10; and finally 5.

When I asked how many people were able to complete this assignment, every woman raised her hand and laughter soon flooded the room.

Next I asked the women to write down 25 things about themselves that was beautiful from the inside out.

Laughter was replaced by gasps, mumbles, and murmurs stating impossibility.

Gibby yelled out from the audience "Ask us to write down 25 things that need to be corrected! We can do that! I have 10 already!" Every woman laughed in agreement and had their pens at the ready to complete the newly suggested activity.

"Take note," I bellowed from the stage. "Most of you look at Gibby and say how stunning she is. Right?" Applause filled the room. I interjected with "But Gibby can't complete this task either. Why is that?"

The answer is simple. Magazine covers tell us the 25 things that we need to correct. While standing in the checkout line at we question our own beauty in comparison to a perfectly airbrushed 17 year old made up to look like a 20 something on magazine covers that are surrounded by words that tell us to be better; like she is?

Enough of comparing yourself against fake flawlessness. Embrace the bold beauty that makes you the woman you are today.

Take Action

Maintaining long straight blonde locks took 400 hours out of my year and $4000 out of my budget. Imagine spending 10 work weeks on your hair and paying for it! I hated my size 14 curves, curly dark hair, and gap toothed smile. After this challenge I learned to love me for me! Will you?

This week I scream BULL$HiT to magazines and dare you to take the challenge.

1: Put a full length mirror in a room where the lighting is great.

2: Put on your make-up, do you

hair, and wear those shoes that make you feel like you are standing on top of the world, and that amazing outfit. Write down 10 things that make you amazing.

3: Strip down to your undies. Keep on the shoes. Write down 10 things that make you feel sexy.

4: Now, take off everything except for the make-up, accessories, and heels. Write down 5 items that make you sexy and stunning.

Tip: If you are struggling with the list; meet your significant other at the door in this birthday suit and heels outfit. I am sure they can help you fill your list.

Week In Review

My greatest challenge this week was:

_____

_____

_____

_____

_____

My greatest success this week was:

_____

_____

_____

_____

_____

I was most challenged when:

_____

_____

_____

_____

_____

I am most proud of:

_____

_____

_____

_____

_____

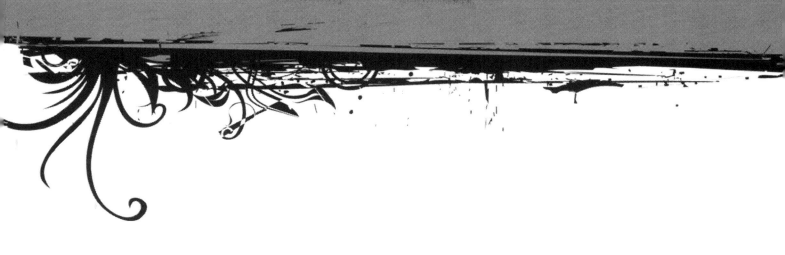

Week of

Reflection

Audacious women:

- ♦ Know life's lessons are meant to be shared.

- ♦ Are not embarrassed by the imperfections, scars, and so-called flaws. These badges of honor show experiences that others have not had the privilege of enjoying.

- ♦ Are open about obstacles, proud of successes, and seek out new challenges every day.

- ♦ Look in the mirror and see the girl that they were, the woman that they are, and their bright future ahead.

Audacious women dare to live a bold, audacious, and unapologetic life.

Reflection

What have you learned about yourself?

_____

_____

_____

_____

_____

The toughest action was:

_____

_____

_____

_____

I have shared my new knowledge with:

_____

_____

_____

_____

_____

The week that I will retry is:

_____

_____

_____

_____

_____

Reflection

My biggest accomplishment was:

_____

_____

_____

_____

_____

What surprised me about myself was:

_____

_____

_____

_____

I am the proudest of myself because:

_____

_____

_____

_____

_____

_____

What I plan to do differently is:

_____

_____

_____

_____

_____

_____

Connect

Reach Out to Dawnna:

Website: www.Dawnna.com or ThinkActEvolve.com

Twitter: http://www.twitter.com/DawnnaStLouis

Facebook: http://www.facebook.com/DawnnaSpeaks

YouTube: http://www.youtube.com/DawnnaSpeaks

Empire Avenue: http://empireavenue.com/Dawnna

LinkedIn: http://www.linkedin.com/Dawnna

More Acts: AudaciousActs.com

Meet Dawnna

Dawnna St Louis follows the tradition of perseverance through adversity to success. Dawnna grew from living in her car right after high-school to a C-Level Executive within 15 years.

Today, Dawnna is considered the preeminent expert on taking action at the crossroads where opportunity and innovation meet. She shares lessons learned from her own adversity to motivate people and companies all over the world to take the next step fearlessly. Where others see risk and fear, Dawnna reveals how to have the guts to move forward. She is bold, audacious, and unapologetic, and consistently brings excitement to every event.

Dawnna creates a whole audience experience that not only drives a message home but actually gets audiences out of their seats and into the action. She shows you how to overcome your own self-limiting beliefs, innovate beyond the octagon (thinking outside the box is so old), and defy what the critics say is possible.

When Dawnna is not traveling the world, you can find her geeking-out on some new techno gadget with her husband and sons.

Made in the USA
Charleston, SC
15 July 2013